Escaping the Courthouse

Private Alternative Dispute Resolution in Los Angeles

Elizabeth Rolph, Erik Moller, Laura Petersen

Supported by the
John Randolph Haynes and Dora Haynes Foundation

THE INSTITUTE FOR CIVIL JUSTICE

The mission of the Institute for Civil Justice is to help make the civil justice system more efficient and more equitable by supplying policymakers and the public with the results of objective, empirically based, analytic research. The ICJ facilitates change in the civil justice system by analyzing trends and outcomes, identifying and evaluating policy options, and bringing together representatives of different interests to debate alternative solutions to policy problems. The Institute builds on a long tradition of RAND research characterized by an interdisciplinary, empirical approach to public policy issues and rigorous standards of quality, objectivity, and independence.

ICJ research is supported by pooled grants from corporations, trade and professional associations, and individuals; by government grants and contracts; and by private foundations. The Institute disseminates its work widely to the legal, business, and research communities, and to the general public. In accordance with RAND policy, all Institute research products are subject to peer review before publication. ICJ publications do not necessarily reflect the opinions or policies of the research sponsors or of the ICJ Board of Overseers.

For more than a decade, the Institute for Civil Justice has been studying alternative dispute resolution (ADR) issues. Early research focused on publicly provided ADR services, especially court-administered arbitration. Recently, attention in the policy community has shifted to private ADR services, and the ICJ has embarked on a series of studies to address issues in this new area.

This report profiles the private alternative dispute resolution market in Los Angeles in an effort to understand that market and its implications for delivery of both public and private dispute resolution.

The study should be of interest to corporations, to corporate law firms interested in the options available for dispute resolution in the private sector, and to decisionmakers who wish to learn more about this growing area of ADR activity.

For information about the Institute for Civil Justice, contact

Dr. Deborah Hensler, Director
Institute for Civil Justice
RAND
1700 Main Street, P.O. Box 2138
Santa Monica, CA 90407-2138
TEL: (310) 451-6916
FAX: (310) 451-6979
Internet: Deborah_Hensler@rand.org

CONTENTS

FIGURES

TABLES

SUMMARY

A growing number of disputants are turning to private resolution mechanisms rather than seeking resolution of their disputes in the courts. This growth is, in turn, raising certain policy questions regarding its implications for the quality of justice in both the public and the private sectors. Our study profiles the private alternative dispute resolution (ADR) market in Los Angeles in an effort to better understand that market and the implications growth may have for the delivery of both public and private dispute resolution.

The data supporting our analysis come from four sources. We interviewed all major private ADR firms in the Los Angeles area. In addition, four of the largest of these firms gave us case-level data, and we obtained case-level data from the Los Angeles Superior Court. We also surveyed private third-party neutrals who are currently listed in area directories as resident in and serving the Los Angeles area.

Our findings suggest that private ADR is an increasingly important component of the Los Angeles dispute resolution marketplace. Although the private caseload currently accounts for only 5 percent of all formal disputes in Los Angeles, it has grown at about 15 percent per year over the last five years, while the public caseload has been more or less stable. Moreover, the disputes going to private ADR are relatively high-value and enduring disputes; 60 percent of those taken to the private sector involve claims exceeding $25,000, contrasting sharply with 14 percent of those in the public sector, and 73 percent proceed to some form of procedural intervention, contrasting with 14 percent in the public sector. Almost half of all private sector disputes are auto personal injury cases. Finally, both businesses and individuals are well represented in the private sector, and insurers appear to play a very important role in bringing disputants to private ADR.

The private sector offers disputants greater procedural variety and typically imposes somewhat higher fees than the courts. Firms and, to a lesser degree, independent neutrals offer a full range of ADR formats, although customers show a marked preference for the traditional format: arbitration. While independent neutrals usually charge clients a simple hourly rate, firms charge both administrative and hearing fees, and in both cases fees are likely to exceed those levied by the courts.

The private sector offers disputants substantial choice among neutrals. The neutrals are generally homogeneous with respect to gender and ethnicity. Seventy-five percent have legal training, and 8 percent are former judges. More than half report they have had some training in ADR techniques. Eight percent of the total pool of neutrals sees over 100 cases per year and accounts for almost 60 percent of the private caseload. Forty-six percent of this group of heavy-hitters are former judges, but in other respects, the heavy-hitters resemble the population of neutrals as a whole.

Our findings have several implications regarding the possible effects private ADR may be expected to have on Los Angeles' courts. Because the private sector currently disposes of only a small fraction of the area's disputes, it cannot be expected to have a significant effect on the workload of the courts. However, since that fraction is likely to grow substantially, private ADR may well lead to a reduced workload in the future. Since the private caseload is small and since almost half the cases are auto personal injury disputes, private ADR does not appear at this point to pose a threat to the public sector's ability to establish precedent and reinforce social norms. At the same time, our findings do not make it clear whether or not the private sector is prematurely stripping the bench of valuable judicial talent.

Our findings also speak to questions regarding the quality of justice in the private sector. In general, neutrals have substantial legal experience and, often, some training in ADR procedures and techniques. At the same time, their role as neutrals is a serious business commitment for many. Because either principal disputants or the insurers who manage their cases return time and again for dispute resolution services, there is at least the apparent *incentive* for neutrals to bias decisions in favor of these repeat customers to maintain their client base. Whether or not there is, in fact, actual bias in the private system deserves further attention.

ACKNOWLEDGMENTS

The authors are indebted to Dan Relles for extensive and invaluable computing and statistical advice throughout the course of this research. We also would like to acknowledge the thoughtful and constructive comments of Rob MacCoun and Craig McEwan, as well as the editorial assistance of Phyllis Gilmore and the secretarial support of Pat Williams. We, of course, take full responsibility for errors of commission as well as omission.

Chapter One

INTRODUCTION

Formal dispute resolution, long thought to be the province of the state, seems to have piqued the interest of the private sector as a possible sphere of activity in recent years. In settings where courts are clogged and criminal cases are forcing civil cases off the calendar, where public juries are perceived as "out of control," and where many are disillusioned with incremental tort reform, a growing number of private individuals are selling their services as neutrals to facilitate dispute resolution. For-profit firms, both independents and national networks, are springing up, positioning themselves in major metropolitan areas. And both new and well-established, nonprofit organizations are actively marketing an expanding array of alternative dispute resolution (ADR) services to an increasingly diverse audience of potential consumers. This flurry of activity springs not from a conscious public decision to privatize the provision of judicial services, but rather from an entrepreneurial intuition that, despite subsidies to the public sector, privately developed portfolios of dispute resolution services can be competitive. Since formal provision of dispute resolution has traditionally been exclusively a public function, the following questions arise: Is there a public interest that should govern in the evolution of this private dispute resolution market? Should this market be encouraged? Should it be regulated? Should it simply be left alone? Shaping sound answers to these difficult questions must reasonably depend first upon developing a clear understanding of the nature of the newly emerging private marketplace.

WHAT IS PRIVATE ALTERNATIVE DISPUTE RESOLUTION?

Because there has been both a growing awareness of the private dispute marketplace and a recent proliferation of services, terminology in this field is new and often inconsistently applied. For example, "private judging" is used by some to refer to all disputes taken to third-party neutrals for some form of counsel or disposition but by others to refer only to that very small subset of cases referred through the courts to a third-party neutral.

For the purposes of this inquiry, we define **private ADR** as

> *any dispute resolution service provided for a fee by a third-party neutral outside the court system.*

Any party that might normally be a party to a dispute may be a disputant in private ADR. Such parties may be businesses, individuals, or government entities—or insurance companies representing principals.

Disputants can come to a private setting by any one of several roads. The dispute can arise in the course of a contractual relationship in which the parties have agreed before the dispute arose to settle any differences through private ADR. Such predispute agreements are increasingly a condition of receiving service in the banking industry and the health care industry;[1] they are also commonly found in employment contracts, construction contracts, and uninsured motorist coverage insurance contracts. Disputants may also agree to take disputes to private ADR after the disputes have arisen, in the belief that they will get a speedier, less-expensive process and a better-reasoned decision. And in some states, disputants may move into private ADR while remaining under the court's jurisdiction. That is, with their case still active in the court, they may choose or the judge may direct them to take the dispute or some phase of its processing, such as discovery, to a private neutral for resolution. Disputants in these "court referenced" cases must pay private fees but usually retain their right to appeal.

---

[1]See "Dispute Resolution Clauses: A Guide for Drafters of Business Agreements" (1994), and Moller and Rolph (1993).

Either in accordance with the terms of the predispute agreement or by mutual agreement, disputants take their dispute to a third-party neutral. This may mean that they take their dispute to a firm that provides private ADR services—usually both administering the disputing process and providing a select panel of neutrals from which the disputants can choose. Such firms include, for example, the American Arbitration Association (AAA) and Judicial Arbitration and Mediation Services (JAMS). Or it may mean that they take their dispute to an independent neutral with no firm affiliation. Because private ADR is usually a matter of choice or private contract, no restrictions or requirements apply to the neutrals. In all instances, fees are privately agreed upon.

Again, because private ADR is typically the product of a contract or an agreement, no rules other than the terms of the agreement govern the nature of the dispute resolution procedure or whether it is binding. Firms and providers are free to offer a full menu of conventional procedures, such as arbitration, mediation, summary jury trials, or fact-finding. They may also create new options that better meet the demands of their clients.

THE POLICY ISSUES

Whether or not private ADR should even enter the range of public scrutiny is the subject of considerable controversy. On the one hand, private ADR is based on a private contractual agreement between parties—a relationship that does not normally command public interest. On the other hand, the provision of dispute resolution, through our public system of justice, is a central function of the state and is closely linked with such important public responsibilities as maintaining order and establishing norms of behavior. Thus, good arguments can be made both supporting and opposing investigation and perhaps ultimate regulation of this new market.

This debate over the private provision of a public service is a recurring theme in public policy (see, for example, Wolf, 1993; Savas, 1982; and Ross, 1988). Some argue in favor of privatization that government is too big and that the private market is more efficient than government at allocating resources. Others counter that equity and distributional concerns require that some services be provided by a public entity. The privatization of judicial services has been a part of this discussion, and the subject of numerous papers (see, for example, Landes and Posner, 1979; Shavell, 1982; Kaplow, 1986; and Cooter and Rubinfeld, 1989).

These arguments aside, private ADR has already divided its ranks of observers. Supporters claim that growth in the private ADR marketplace will benefit both the public and the user communities. These supporters argue that, by diverting cases to the private sector, private ADR will reduce the growing burdens on the public courts, which, in turn, will reduce public costs and allow the courts to offer better, faster service to those disputants that remain. At the same time, the supporters assert that private ADR can provide disputants with faster, less expensive processes that can be tailored to their particular needs and that are managed by experienced neutrals. In addition, private ADR offers a private setting for dispute resolution, which, supporters allege, is less stressful and is likely to facilitate resolution (see Galanter and Lande, 1992).

Opponents, on the other hand, argue that private ADR serves neither public nor private interests well. They prophesy that movement of business and insurance disputes from the public into a private setting will lead to the further erosion of financial support for public judicial services and will create a system that offers two-tiered justice to the privileged few. Private ADR will also, opponents believe, strip the bench of its best and most experienced judicial talent, as good judges leave for the higher wages and better working conditions of the private sector. Moreover, because private ADR proceedings and decisions are not public, society will be deprived of cases that may be valuable vehicles for establishing precedent and articulating behavioral norms. For their part, disputants in the private sector will be deprived of many of the procedural safeguards, such as the right to appeal, offered in the public sector. Opponents also argue that neutrals, who may be anxious to please customers and thus "build a practice," have strong incentives to rule in favor of disputants who offer the best prospect of repeat business (see, for example, Reuben, 1994, and Galanter and Lande, 1992).

At the moment, arguments on both sides of the question are speculative. The private ADR market is new, and we have very little empirical information to provide sound bases for exploring the very complex questions raised in the arguments. The purpose of this study is to begin to bridge that gap.

STUDY FOCUS AND RESEARCH QUESTIONS

As a first step in laying the groundwork for further explorations, we must equip ourselves with a basic descriptive understanding of the nature of the private ADR marketplace. That market breaks into three important components:

- Consumers: disputants and their disputes

- The product: ADR services and price

- Producers: neutrals supplying ADR services.

In this report, after summarizing the broad outlines of the market, we will examine the characteristics of consumers of private ADR, focusing especially on caseload characteristics including volume, seriousness of dispute, and types of disputes. We also examine the availability of ADR procedures, the frequency with which they may be used, and the market's fee structure. Finally, we look more closely at the provider community, exploring the relevant characteristics of third-party neutrals—both independent neutrals and neutrals serving on firm panels.

METHODS AND DATA SOURCES

To allow us to explore these questions in some depth, we have narrowed our focus of attention to a well-defined population of cases and to a single geographical area.

We have chosen Los Angeles as the study site. Los Angeles is a major metropolitan area with a large and diverse court caseload (see Kakalik, Selvin, and Pace, 1990). The Los Angeles Superior Court is also a court the Institute for Civil Justice has studied extensively, giving us valuable data for comparing public and private caseloads (see Kakalik, Selvin, and Pace, 1990). At the same time, the anecdotal evidence suggests that Los Angeles has an active and rapidly growing private ADR marketplace, that it is on the "cutting edge." Thus, what we learn from this study should be predictive of what other regions will experience in the future.

We limit our population of cases by type and time, as well. Our analysis captures all civil money disputes. It specifically excludes family law, probate, and other types of disputes that fall outside of that definition. The analysis is also cross-sectional, including only cases and service providers that were active in 1992 and 1993. Although a longitudinal study would have permitted us to identify direction and degree of change in the volatile marketplace, data from both the providing firms and the independent neutrals unfortunately would not support this more ambitious format.

Our analysis is based primarily on data from four sources: open-ended interviews with firms providing private ADR services, case records from a subset of those firms, a survey of all third-party neutrals offering services in the Los Angeles area, and Los Angeles County Superior Court case records.[2]

Firm Interviews

In an initial screening survey, we contacted 22 firms offering private ADR services in the Los Angeles area.[3] Using information regarding size, caseload, and type of cases gathered, we selected the six most active firms—between them handling approximately 60 percent of the private civil caseload—and returned to them for complete interviews. These six firms supplied both descriptive interview information and marketing materials on their histories, services, and practices. These six firms supplied both descriptive interview information and marketing materials on their history, services, and practices.

---

[2]This information was supplemented by information provided in the Annual Data Reference publications of the Judicial Council of California.

[3]The ADR firms offering services in the Los Angeles area were originally identified and contacted in 1992. We updated the 1992 list and contacted the firms again in 1993, eliminating those that did not provide services that conform with our definition of private ADR and adding new firms that had entered the market during the intervening year.

Firm Case Records

Of these six firms, three agreed to make case-level data files for the year 1992 available for this study, and a fourth agreed to provide us with aggregate caseload information that we specified.[4]

Survey of Neutrals

In addition to collecting information from firms providing private ADR, we conducted a mail and telephone survey of the neutrals who provide services in the Los Angeles area, to gather information regarding both their patterns of practice and the characteristics of disputes that came directly to them. The timing of the mail survey was such that we asked for information about each of the disputes that came to them during the first seven months of 1993, assuming that this information would be comparable to firm case-level data collected in 1992.[5] We mailed questionnaires to all those identified by the firms we contacted as members of their provider panels. In one case, the firm's panel list included almost 1,200 names, so we randomly sampled from this list.[6] Otherwise, all panel members were surveyed. In addition, we sent questionnaires to all individuals not already identified as panel members who were listed in the "Private Judges" and "Arbitrators and Mediators" sections of the 1992 Directory of California Lawyers as serving the Los Angeles area, the local telephone directory, or advertisements, as providing ADR for civil cases. There was substantial overlap among the various lists; ultimately, we sent questionnaires to 715 potential respondents. One hundred and seventy-four were categorized as "ineligible"; that is, they either had not served as a neutral sometime during the previous five years or were deceased. Of the remaining 541 individuals, 48 percent of the eligible population responded through the mail ques-

---

[4]One of the largest of the companies supplied us with five years of data, hoping we could ultimately conduct a longitudinal analysis. The others either were newly launched or did not have computerized records predating 1991.

[5]Respondents were likely to be referring to their daily calendars for information on cases. To ensure high-quality data and a good response rate, we asked only about disputes respondents heard in 1993— the year they received the questionnaire.

[6]In this case, the firm lists its entire membership as potential neutrals, despite the fact that many do not provide neutral services.

tionnaire, and that response rate was increased to 76 percent through follow-up telephone interviews.[7] All completed surveys were weighted for the analysis and our results indicate that there are about 1,200 neutrals serving the Los Angeles area.

To determine whether or not the respondent populations for the mail and telephone surveys were different, we compared respondent characteristics and found no systematic bias. We also checked responses to selected questions for internal consistency, which we found to be high.

Superior Court Case Records

Finally, to compare characteristics of the public and private caseloads, we obtained Los Angeles Superior Court case records for all civil matters opened between 1988 and 1992. This data set includes information on the parties, the type of action, the filing and disposition dates, and the type of disposition.

ORGANIZATION

This report is organized according to the research areas listed above. In Chapter Two, we broadly describe the private ADR marketplace in Los Angeles. In Chapter Three, we present information on the characteristics of the ADR caseload and of the disputants. In Chapter Four, we describe both the ADR services offered and those used by disputants and examine the pricing structures of the firms and the independent neutrals. In Chapter Five, we develop a profile of the third-party neutral population, and, in the final chapter, we review our findings and draw conclusions that bear on some of the policy issues raised above.

---

[7]A few questions were omitted from the telephone survey to shorten the response time required. Otherwise the questions were the same.

Chapter Two

LOS ANGELES' PRIVATE ADR MARKETPLACE—AN OVERVIEW

HISTORY OF PRIVATE ADR

Prior to the mid-1800s, the nation's courts were hostile to infringement of their dispute resolution jurisdiction. From 1854, the year of an important U.S. Supreme Court decision in support of arbitration,[1] through the early 1900s, the courts' resolve was tested by ADR proponents, but the courts' hold on dispute resolution services was unwavering. Finally, in 1920, New York passed laws validating arbitration agreements that paved the way for the development of private ADR nationwide.[2]

Two major developments that followed closely on the heels of the New York Arbitration Act were the passage of the Federal Arbitration Act (FAA)[3] and the establishment of the American Arbitration Association (AAA). With the passage of the FAA, virtually every state and the federal government followed New York's lead, adopting some form of arbitration act. The AAA, in turn, provided a vehicle for realizing the goals of these adjudicatory reforms.

However, it was not until the 1960s that the evolution became a revolution. In 1960, the U.S. Supreme Court published a series of decisions interpreting the FAA and establishing a strong public policy fa-

---

[1] *Burchell v. March*, 58 U.S. 344, 349–350 (1854).

[2] New York Arbitration Act, N.Y. Civ. Prac. L.& R. 7501–7514 (1980 & Supp. 1986).

[3] 9 U.S.C. § 1, *et seq.* (1988 & Supp. 1991).

voring arbitration.[4] In the 30 years since these opinions, the Court has continued broadening its support for arbitration.[5] Currently, the Court allows arbitrators broad powers in deciding virtually any case.

During this same period, there has been a decline in our capacity to resolve disputes informally, while the grounds for formal disputing have expanded. These trends have lead to an overcrowding of the nation's courts, and jurists, legal scholars, and legislatures have looked for alternatives, including private ADR, to relieve some of the courts' burden. As a result, ADR procedures, particularly arbitration and mediation, have been broadly integrated into both the public and private sectors, serving as the framework for court-annexed programs and judicial settlement efforts.

PRIVATE ADR IN CALIFORNIA

Many of these national trends played out in California. In the late 1970s, California introduced a court-annexed arbitration program in which cases in certain jurisdictions were subject to mandatory non-binding arbitration.[6] Simultaneously, California common law followed federal law, offering broad support to private arbitration. This support takes two forms. First, the courts have substantially narrowed the grounds for appealing a binding arbitration decision, making arbitration decisions final and binding on the parties.[7] Second, California courts have generally upheld the validity of predispute arbitration clauses.[8]

---

[4]*United Steelworkers v. American Mfg.*, 363 U.S. 564 (1960); *United Steelworkers v. Warrior & Gulf Nav. Co.*, 363 U.S. 574 (1960); *United Steelworkers v. Enterprise Wheel & Car Co.*, 363 U.S. 583 (1960).

[5]See, e.g., *Sherck v. Alberto-Culver Co.*, 417 U.S. 506 (1974); *Mitsubishi Motors Co. v. Soler Chrysler-Plymouth, Inc.*, 473 U.S. 614 (1984); *Gilmer v. Interstate/Johnson Lane Corp.*, 500 U.S. 20, 111 S. Ct. 1647 (1991).

[6]Cal. Civ. Proc. Code §§ 1141.10, *et seq.* (1992).

[7]See, e.g., *Moncharsh v. Heily & Blase*, 3 Cal. 4th 1 (1992). See also Cal. Civ. Proc. Code § 1286.2 (1994). This situation raises many concerns among the critics of the widespread use of private ADR. They argue that disputants lose the ability to remedy mistakes of fact or law, which exists through the appellate process in the public courts, and that the quality of private ADR may be suspect because of this failing.

[8]See, e.g., *Moncharsh, supra* note 12. See also Cal. Civ. Proc. Code § 1281 (1994).

As a result, there has been an explosion in private ADR in California. The simultaneous growth in formal disputing, incorporation of ADR into the menu of public dispute resolution services, and legal support for private ADR outcomes has created a fertile environment for the development of a private ADR marketplace. This is perhaps nowhere more obvious than in Los Angeles.

The Los Angeles market now hosts a growing number of providers, each attempting to take advantage of the hospitable climate for private ADR. These providers take several forms. They may be firms or lone individuals; if they are firms, they are likely to vary along important dimensions, including location, size, age, profit or nonprofit status, organizational structure, and marketing and business strategy.

Firm ADR Providers in Los Angeles

We identified 22 firms providing ADR services in Los Angeles County. After an initial screening process, we concluded that 13 of these firms are outside the scope of this study, because the services they provide do not conform with our definition of private ADR. These excluded firms include a local bar association, the Better Business Bureau, and national referral organizations.[9] Table 2.1 lists the remaining nine firms that offer private services for the disposition of civil money disputes in Los Angeles County.[10] These firms differ in size, location, age, organizational structure, and marketing and business strategy.

Table 2.1 presents the important characteristics of the nine firms. The providers include five large[11] national companies and four local companies, all with varying market shares. Some firms have numerous offices, both in Los Angeles County and outside Southern California. In general, the firms based outside of Los Angeles are larger than the local firms, although local firms are increasing their

---

[9]See Appendix A.

[10]As previously described, we subsequently returned to the six firms that are actually providing private ADR services in Los Angeles County for the data we describe in this report.

[11]Our definition of size is based on number of cases, number of providers, and amount of revenue. To maintain the anonymity of our sources, we do not provide these data, but instead present an indicator of relative size based on these data.

Table 2.1
Los Angeles County Private ADR Firm Providers

Firm	Headquarters	Profit	Administrative Employees	Year Founded	Size	Local Market	Market
Alternative Resolution Centers	Los Angeles, CA	Profit	6	1987	Medium	Medium	General Business
American Arbitration Association	New York, NY	Non-Profit	45	1926 in LA	Large	Large	General Business
Arbitration Forums, Inc.	Tampa, FL	Non-Profit	4.5	1964 in LA	Large	Small	Insurance—insurance subrogation actions
Arts Arbitration and Mediation Service	San Francisco, CA	Non-Profit	1.5	1986 in LA	Small	Small	Limited to arts-related disputes
First Mediation Corporation	Los Angeles, CA	Profit	6	1991	Medium	Medium	Insurance/Tort
J.A.M.S., Inc.	Orange, CA	Profit	19	1979 in LA	Large	Large	General Business
Judicate, Inc.	Lake Success, NY	Profit	14	1992 in LA	Large	Medium	Insurance/Tort
Real Estate Mediation and Arbitration	Los Angeles, CA	Profit	1	1990	Small	Small	Limited to real estate related disputes
United States Arbitration and Mediation, Inc.	Seattle, WA	Profit	8	1992 in LA	Large	Small	Insurance/Tort

SOURCES: Publicly available information and confidential interview information.

NOTE: Our definition of size is based on number of cases, number of providers, and amount of revenue. To maintain the anonymity of our sources, we do not provide these data, but instead present an indicator of relative size based on these data.

market shares. Some of the nine firms are well-established, and some are new firms. The first firm opened an office in Southern California in 1926. However, it was not until 1964 that the second organization appeared, with others following in the late 1980s and early 1990s. Three of the firms are nonprofit and six are for-profit. Currently, only one of the companies is a publicly traded corporation.

Local staffing generally varies with the size of the firm. Firms usually employ only administrative staff and provide their dispute resolution services through nonexclusive independent contracts with retired judges, attorneys, and nonattorneys. Only rarely will firms employ neutrals as members of their staffs. However, one large firm uses only exclusive contracts in retaining its panel of neutrals, while others may selectively employ exclusive contracts.

Marketing strategies differ among the firms. In the past, firms did not narrowly prescribe their business specialties, but recently, they have begun specializing in particular types of disputes, with tailored marketing efforts. For example, Real Estate Arbitration and Mediation, Inc., established in 1990, specializes in real estate–related disputes. Other recently established firms specialize in insurance and tort disputes. Traditional firm marketing tools include advertising, seminars, directory listings, and cold-calling prospective clients.

Independent Neutral Providers in Los Angeles

Independent neutral providers are an integral part of the Los Angeles private ADR marketplace, handling over half the disputes brought to that sector.[12] The total number of independent neutrals providing private ADR services in Los Angeles County is about 1,200.[13] These neutrals have a broad range of backgrounds, market shares, ages, interests, and business and marketing strategies.[14] They often play a

---

[12]See Chapter Three, Table 3.1.

[13]This figure includes those individuals we identified through the procedures described in the Introduction. It is probable that there are a small number of individuals who live outside of the Los Angeles area and do not advertise or otherwise market themselves in Los Angeles who nonetheless serve the area.

[14]See Chapter Four.

dual role, hearing both disputes that are brought to them directly and disputes that are brought to them through firms on whose panels they serve.[15] Eighty-eight percent of the neutrals list themselves as being on at least one panel.

The most prevalent form of marketing for neutrals is word of mouth (cited by 50 percent of the neutrals in our survey).[16] Only 11 percent claim to advertise their services.[17] Eighty-six percent of the neutrals state that they have additional employment besides ADR, which probably offers these respondents an additional venue for attracting business.[18]

Neutrals claim to specialize both in the types of disputes they handle and the types of procedures they offer to a greater extent than do the firms. Forty-one percent of the neutrals claim to specialize in a particular form of private ADR service. In addition, 68 percent state that they specialize in a particular type of dispute. In contrast, only two of the nine firms stated a similar concentration.

This brief history and description of the structure of Los Angeles' private ADR providers should serve as the backdrop for our exploration of that market in the sections that follow.

---

[15]Some firms, however, require or negotiate exclusive agreements with the neutrals on their panels on a case-by-case basis.

[16]Survey of Alternative Dispute Resolution Services (hereinafter "Survey"), Question 36.

[17]Survey, Question 36.

[18]Survey, Question 3.

Chapter Three

THE DEMAND SIDE: DISPUTES AND DISPUTANTS

Renewed interest in private ADR has been the direct result of perceptions that it is a growing phenomenon and that, in some reasonable period of time, it will account for a significant share of the dispute resolution delivered. Only as it achieves some presence in the market can private ADR have any meaningful effect, for better or worse, on the public judicial system or on disputants collectively. However, it must be stressed that the growing interest is based on "perceptions." Because this is a private market, there are no public records to document changes in use, and the decentralized and often sketchy information that exists in the private sector is generally very tightly held.

In this chapter, we draw on information collected from firms providing private ADR services, from neutrals, and from the Los Angeles courts to profile the caseload and the disputants using private ADR services and to compare private-sector with public-sector use. A number of characteristics are of particular interest, because they bear most directly on current policy debates. They include the following:

- **Volume**—The size of the private caseload is important in that it suggests the limits of costs and/or benefits that currently result from private ADR. If, contrary to popular belief, very few cases are going to private resolution, there may be less likelihood that private activity is affecting the public sector, and there need be less concern with the costs and benefits it may bestow on users.

- **Growth rate**—Like volume, growth rate is an important measure of the likelihood that the private sector is or will in the future be a

15

significant component of the dispute resolution marketplace. It is particularly important as a window into the future role of the private sector.

- **Value of disputes**—Case value is one measure of the importance of a case and of the likelihood that the case will occupy some court time. ADR is sometimes associated with "little cases"— cases that, without the simpler, less expensive ADR option, would not be pursued. If private ADR is composed principally of these "little cases," it may not be absorbing the cases that actually consume public court time and resources.

- **Durability of disputes**—Durability of disputes refers to the likelihood that a case will proceed to some kind of third-party intervention. It is used as a second indicator of the seriousness of a dispute and the likelihood that it will consume court time.

- **Types of cases**—Case type refers to the class of civil dispute being pursued, e.g., personal injury, employment, or medical malpractice. Knowing the proportions of different types of cases that go to private ADR not only gives us further insight into the importance of various classes of disputes to the overall caseload, it also may help identify ADR's particular appeal and bound our projections of future growth.

- **Types of disputants**—For this analysis, we classify disputants as individuals or businesses based on their listed names in the case record. A corollary of the argument that ADR attracts small cases is that it attracts novice disputants—those who would not be pursuing their disputes but for the availability of a less expensive, less imposing process. If this is true, a disproportionate number of disputants are likely to be individuals. On the other hand, some argue, to the contrary, that private ADR offers experienced disputants an efficient, friendly environment in which to pursue their disputes—perhaps even an environment so eager to see their return that heavy users receive favored treatment. If the latter scenario is more the measure of reality, we might expect to see disproportionate numbers of businesses, especially larger businesses.

We characterize the private ADR disputes and disputants on these dimensions and conclude with a brief discussion of the various routes by which they may get to private ADR—the all-important gatekeeping function.

VOLUME

Volume is, perhaps, the most obvious measure of the importance of the private ADR caseload. Speculation and anecdotes aside, how many disputes is this alternative system of justice actually handling, and what fraction of Los Angeles' total dispute caseload does that encompass?

To address these questions, we constructed a measure of the total ADR caseload by adding all disputes that neutrals reported handling both through firms and independent of firms[1] and compared that number with caseload reports for Los Angeles Superior, Municipal, and Small Claims Courts published by the California Judicial Council.

Table 3.1 shows that, of the total 465,578 disputes filed in Los Angeles during 1993, an overwhelming 95 percent were resolved in the public sector (small claims, municipal, and superior courts). The remainder were split between firms and independent neutrals handling cases that come directly to them. In reality, our analysis slightly underestimates the proportion of disputes that are being disposed of by the private sector, because a substantial number of those disputes have also been filed in the public sector before they go to the private sector. Firms and independent neutrals often do not know the status of disputes that they handle, and our respondents were only able to identify the status of 71 percent of their caseload. Of these disputes, respondents report that 72 percent had been filed in the public courts before being brought to the private sector. If we apply this same percentage to the total private caseload, it suggests that the private sector may account for 5.3 percent of the total dispute caseload, which is not a meaningful difference.

---

[1]To confirm the accuracy of these reported data, we compared the neutrals' estimates with data from cooperating firms and found the two consistent. See Appendix A.

Table 3.1

**Distribution of Disputes Between the Public and
Private Sectors in 1993**

	Number of Claims Filed	Percentage of Total
Courts (superior, municipal, and small claims)[a]	441,906	94.9
Private ADR		
Firms[b]	12,941	2.8
Independent[b] neutrals	10,731	2.3
Total	23,672	5.1
Total disputes	465,578	100.0

[a]Data from Judicial Council of California (1994).
[b]Survey, Question 13.

If one looks only at volume, it is hard to describe private ADR as a major player in dispute resolution. But volume should not be the only measure of importance.

GROWTH IN THE PRIVATE SECTOR

A second measure of the role private ADR can be expected to play in delivering justice is its growth rate. To determine the growth rate, we asked neutrals in our survey how many private civil disputes they had handled in each of the years from 1988 to 1993. However, simply determining the rate of growth in the private sector does not tell us whether private ADR is increasing its share of the total caseload, maintaining a stable share, or perhaps receiving a declining market share in the context of a very rapid general increase in disputing. To provide a baseline against which to measure changes in reported private ADR activity,[2] we also compare the experience in the private sector with changes in the number of cases filed in the Los Angeles courts over that same period.

Figure 3.1 shows that the private ADR caseload in Los Angeles grew steadily at an average rate of about 15 percent per year between 1988

---

[2]We specifically asked respondents to report only private disputes and exclude any court-annexed cases that they might have handled.

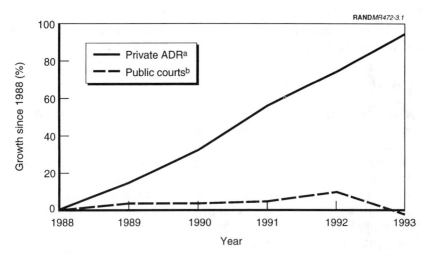

RAND*MR472-3.1*

aSurvey, Questions 11 and 13.
bJudicial Council of California (1989–1994).

Figure 3.1—Percentage of Growth Since 1988

and 1993,[3] which is in sharp contrast to the public caseload, which actually decreased at –0.5 percent between 1988 and 1993. Even in 1993, when the public caseload shrank by over 50,000 cases, private ADR continued to account for a growing number of disputes resolved. These results attest to the fact that the Los Angeles market for private ADR, although certainly small, young, and, no doubt, still vulnerable, has experienced both strong and steady growth over the last several years. Since no current evidence suggests a substantial change in relative growth rates of the courts and the private sector, private ADR may well become a significant feature in the judicial

---

[3]We recognize that our numbers probably overestimate the growth somewhat, but not a great deal. Some who provided services in earlier years are no longer available to answer our survey. Our estimate for the private caseload in 1988, for example, is, in all likelihood, lower than the actual private caseload. Also, because we asked respondents about cases that they had "handled" in a given year, there is some small possibility that a few disputes straddled two years and were counted twice. We do not think this very likely, both because disputes that go to the private sector do not remain active for long periods and because respondents understood that we were interested in numbers of cases.

landscape. If one extrapolates current ADR growth trends against a stable population of disputes, private ADR could resolve as many as 13 percent of the area's disputes by the year 2000.

VALUE OF DISPUTES

Alternative dispute resolution is frequently believed to be a good way to dispose of small cases—cases that deserve a hearing but do not warrant the court's time.[4] Consistent with that view, research into the effects of judicial arbitration suggests that the availability of court programs may well increase the number of small cases filed, because litigants see the opportunity for a less formal, less expensive hearing.[5] Thus, we might expect that private ADR provides a similar opportunity in the private sector and that, rather than resolving more substantial cases that would otherwise be consuming court time and resources, private ADR would generate its own demand in the community of small-stakes claimants who would not have pursued their claims in the courts. Surprisingly, both our claim and award data provide evidence to the contrary.

We combined individual claims data from one large firm with similar data from our survey of neutrals.[6] As Table 3.2 shows, the amount in question was greater than $25,000 in 60 percent of these disputes as compared with 14 percent in the public court caseload ($p < 0.01$).[7] Although our estimate may be somewhat high because the one firm that supplied claims data handled a higher-stakes caseload than most other firms, any reasonable adjustment would still show a substantial difference between public and private claim amounts.

Furthermore, of the private caseload, the cases that do not go to firms but, rather, go directly to neutrals are by far the highest-stakes

---

[4]National Center for State Courts/State Justice Institute (1994).

[5]Id.

[6]Firms often do not keep claim information, and only one firm in our group could supply it.

[7]This percentage constitutes the proportion of the total Los Angeles caseload that is filed in Superior Court, which requires as one of its sources of jurisdiction that the amount in contest be $25,000 or more.

Table 3.2

Distribution of Disputes ≥ $25,000

	Total Number of Cases	Number of Cases ≥ $25,000	Percentage of Cases
Private caseload	11,340	6,783	60
Firm[a]	—	—	31
Independent neutrals[b]	—	—	69
All Los Angeles courts[c]	441,906	61,438	14

[a]Case-level data from one firm for 1992. Numbers of cases not presented to protect identity of firm.

[b]Survey, Question 29.

[c]Superior Court caseload (1993); Judicial Council (1993).

group of all, with claim amounts of $25,000 or more reported for 69 percent of the cases. Figure 3.2 shows how disputes going directly to independent neutrals are distributed across the range of values.

The conclusion that serious disputes account for a substantial share of the private caseload generally held up as we examined awards, although we found marked differences in the award distribution both among the firms and between the firms and the independent neutrals. Figure 3.3 shows that cases resolved through firms have substantially lower award amounts than cases that go directly to neutrals. The fact that 66 percent of the cases handled through firms receive a defense verdict, in contrast to only 16 percent of those handled directly by neutrals (p < 0.01), suggests that liability is generally less clear in disputes resolved through firms, as well.[8]

Survey results suggest that the value of private ADR disputes is increasing. Slightly less than half of the neutrals who responded to our survey thought the values of their caseloads had increased over the

---

[8]In addition to variation between cases that go to firms and those that go directly to neutrals, there is also substantial variation across firms in the percentage of disputes that receive a defense verdict.

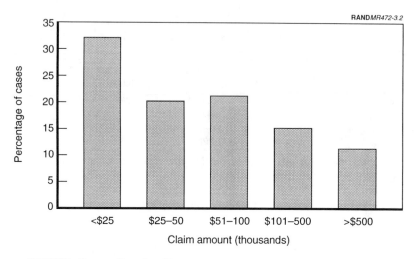

SOURCE: Survey, Question 29.

Figure 3.2—Claim Amounts for Non-Firm Disputes

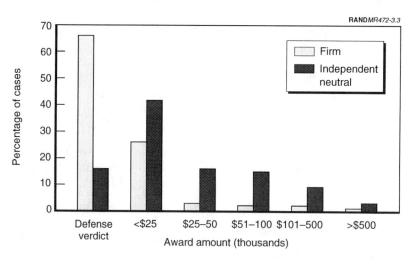

SOURCE: Firm case level data; Survey, Question 30.

Figure 3.3—Size of Awards for Firms and Independent Neutrals

last five years, while a similar number thought it had remained the same, and only 9 percent thought it had declined.[9]

DURABILITY OF DISPUTES

Disputes going to private ADR are not only comparatively high-value disputes, they appear to be durable disputes—disputes that ultimately require third-party intervention. Table 3.3 shows that 73 percent of all private ADR disputes continue to some form of third-party intervention (an arbitration hearing, a mediation, a mini-trial, etc.). This offers sharp contrast to the 14 percent of all Superior Court filings that ever reach a settlement conference. Perhaps many disputants only seek out private ADR when they conclude that they cannot reach bilateral settlement. Table 3.3 also shows the substantial variation among firms. This may be, at least in part, attributable to differences in firm filing or administrative fees, which are levied when a dispute is brought to a firm and can be quite substantial (Chapter Four).

Table 3.3

Percentage of Cases That Go to Third-Party Intervention

Private ADR		
Firms		
Firm 1	68	
Firm 2	90	
Firm 3	46	
Total[a]	78	
Independent neutrals[b]	70	
Total private ADR		73
Superior Court[c]		14

[a]Firm case-level data.
[b]Survey, Question 28.
[c]Kakalik (1990). This is the percentage of Superior Court cases that remained in the system long enough to reach the mandatory settlement conference procedure, which involves considerable judicial intervention with the parties.

---

[9]This question was on the mailed questionnaire but was not part of the telephone interview. Therefore, respondents who answered questions in the phone interview are not part of this summary.

TYPES OF DISPUTES

Although we are unable to make exact comparisons of the mix of disputes brought to the public and the private sectors, because we do not have precisely comparable data, our data suggest that their respective caseloads are quite different.[10] Using the Judicial Council case type categories, Table 3.4 shows that the private sector has a substantially higher proportion of auto personal injury cases than does the Superior Court (43 versus 29 percent) and somewhat lower proportions of other personal injury cases and other civil complaints ($p < 0.01$). It seems unlikely, although possible, that these differences would disappear if we were to incorporate the Municipal and Small Claims cases.

The difference in caseload composition can, at least in part, be explained by private ADR firms aggressively targeting the auto insurance companies in their marketing. Our firm interviews suggest these companies offer a welcome opportunity to develop relationships with point sources for continuing streams of future cases. Persuading corporate disputants to name a particular firm or a firm's procedural rules in widely used predispute contracts can accomplish the same end. AAA and JAMS, for example, are widely known to use this tool aggressively in their marketing.

Table 3.4

Case Type by Sector
(percent)

	Private[a]	Courts[b]
Civil complaints	41	46
Auto personal injury	43	29
Other personal injury	16	26

[a]Firm case-level data; Survey, Question 26.

[b]Superior Court Caseload (1993); Judicial Council (1994).

---

[10]There is no publicly available information on the types of disputes that make up the total caseload of the Los Angeles courts. However, the California Judicial Council does report the Los Angeles County Superior Court's caseload broken into three major types of disputes.

The private ADR caseload itself has several interesting characteristics that suggest that private ADR attracts particular types of disputes and that firms and independent providers play somewhat different roles in the marketplace.

Table 3.5, column 3, shows that the rates at which types of disputes are brought into the private sector vary and confirms the predominance of auto personal injury, which accounts for 42 percent of all cases brought to private ADR. There are several explanations for this distribution. It may simply reflect the underlying case-type population. In addition, however, ADR may be thought to be more appropriate for some types of cases than for others. Since attorneys or insurers, acting as procedural gatekeepers, are likely to play a major role in directing disputes to ADR, variation may also be explained by gatekeeper preferences. For example, those who handle the auto personal injury may also be more familiar and more comfortable with ADR procedures than those who handle other types of cases and might, therefore, take their cases to ADR more frequently.

Case mixes vary not only between firms and independents ($p < 0.01$) but also among firms. For example, Table 3.5, columns 1 and 2, show

Table 3.5

Comparison of Firm and Independent Case Mix[a]
(percent)

	Firm[b]	Independent[c]	Total Private
Auto personal injury[d]	36	46	42
Employment	8	16	12
Other contract	20	9	13
Non-auto personal injury	13	6	9
Construction	10	4	7
Real property	7	5	6
Malpractice	2	5	4

[a]Case categories with fewer than 3 percent of the caseload omitted.

[b]Firm case-level data.

[c]Survey, Question 26.

[d]Private auto personal injury differs between Tables 3.4 and Table 3.5 because of rounding.

that auto personal injury, malpractice, and employment disputes play a more prominent role in the caseload of independent neutrals than of firms. Independent neutrals also seem more likely to attract types of disputes that are typically of higher value (see Table 3.3). Variations among firms can also be substantial. For example, construction cases make up 23 percent of one large firm's caseload, while only one other firm handles any (1 percent of its caseload).[11] These differences probably reflect the targeted marketing strategies of firms, each seeking a profitable market niche. Independent neutrals as a group, on the other hand, handle a broad caseload.

To determine whether or not the case mix is changing, we asked the providers, both firms and independent neutrals, if they have observed any changes in the mix over the past few years. Respondents generally agree that little change has taken place; firms report no changes, and very few of the independent neutrals responded to this question. The few neutrals who have observed change note a relatively greater number of auto personal injury and employment cases.[12]

Only three of the cooperating firms provided us with data on the awards for all cases within each category of disputes. Not surprisingly, we found that the award amounts of cases vary with the type of dispute. Table 3.6a shows that a defense verdict is reached in 95 percent of the employment disputes, while only 23 percent of the consumer disputes are decided with a defense verdict. At the same time, Table 3.6b shows that auto personal injury disputes account for almost a quarter (24 percent) of disputes in which awards are less than $25,000, and employment disputes account for the greatest share of defense verdicts (20 percent).

DISPUTANT CHARACTERISTICS

Available measures of disputant characteristics are all extremely imperfect indicators both of the sophistication of the disputant as a

---

[11]To preserve confidentiality, we cannot report the breakdown of case types by individual firms.

[12]Survey, Question 27.

Table 3.6a

Distribution of Award Amounts Within Case-Type Categories for Three Firms (percent)

Case Types	Defense Verdict	0–$25K	$25–50K	$50–100K	$100–500K	>$500K
			Award Amounts			
Construction	51	35	6	3	3	1
Auto personal injury	53	43	3	1	0	0
Employment	95	4	0	0	0	0
Real property	55	37	4	3	1	1
Other contract	62	22	6	5	3	2
Other personal injury	71	23	3	2	1	0
Unknown	66	22	4	2	5	1
Other	88	8	3	1	1	0
Consumer	23	77	0	0	0	0
Product liability	50	50	0	0	0	0
Other tort	67	33	0	0	0	0
Total distribution of award amounts	63	29	4	2	2	1

SOURCE: Survey, Questions 26 and 30.
NOTE: Percentages may not sum to 100 because of rounding.

Table 3.6b

Distribution of Case Types Within Award-Amount Categories for Three Firms (percent)

Case Types	Defense Verdict	0–$25K	$25–50K	$50–100K	$100–500K	>$500K	Total Distribution of Case Types
			Award Amounts				
Construction	15	23	30	29	31	35	19
Auto personal injury	14	24	14	4	4	0	16
Employment	20	2	2	3	0	6	13
Real property	11	17	13	17	9	12	13
Other contract	11	9	20	26	20	35	11
Other personal injury	13	9	9	11	9	0	11
Unknown	9	7	9	8	26	12	8
Other	6	1	3	1	2	0	4
Consumer	1	8	0	0	0	0	3
Product liability	0	0	0	0	0	0	0
Other tort	0	0	0	0	0	0	0

SOURCE: Survey, Questions 26 and 30.
NOTE: Percentages may not sum to 100 because of rounding.

consumer of ADR services and of what brought that disputant to private ADR. However, the relative proportions of businesses and individuals in the disputing population may at least suggest whether private ADR is becoming the exclusive domain of businesses attempting to cut litigation costs and circumvent juries or, alternatively, of individual disputants anxious to pursue disputes in what they may believe is a less expensive, friendlier setting.

To determine how often individuals and businesses dispute in public and private forums, we identified as individuals or businesses the principal plaintiffs and defendants in a random sample of Superior Court cases[13] and a census of private ADR cases. Table 3.7 shows that both businesses and individuals are well represented in the private and the public forums. The significantly ($p < 0.01$) larger percentage of business-versus-business disputes in the private sector suggests that private ADR is particularly attractive to business disputants.

Businesses may force individuals into private ADR through predispute contract clauses when the business is either the plaintiff/claimant or the defendant/respondent in a dispute. For this reason, we aggregated into one category all disputes in which a disputant on one side of the dispute is an individual and a disputant on the other side of the dispute is a business entity.

Table 3.7

**Disputant Types: Public and Private Sectors
(percent)**

	Courts[a]	Private ADR[b]
Individual vs. individual	38	43
Mixed	45	29
Business vs. business	17	29

NOTE: Percentages may not sum to 100 because of rounding.
[a]Los Angeles County Superior Court case-level data.
[b]Firm case-level data; Survey, Question 20.

---

[13]We selected a random sample of 4,335 (from a total of 26,507) 1992 Los Angeles Superior Court cases from which to identify disputants.

Obscured by the identification of disputants is the fact that insurance companies also play a substantial role in disputes that are nominally between individuals, and some portion of the disputes between "individuals" in the private sector may well reflect business (e.g., insurer) rather than individual preferences. Our survey respondents report that insurance companies represented one or more of the parties in 69 percent of the disputes that came to them directly.[14] They also report, as we have noted in Table 3.5, that almost half of these cases are automobile personal injury disputes, cases in which it is common practice for the individual represented by an insurance company to be the named party. Given this practice, it is likely that Table 3.7 substantially underreports business involvement.

In sum, we have found that the private market for dispute resolution serves a small but growing proportion of Los Angeles' formal disputes; these disputes are not small, but rather reasonably high-value and durable disputes; a high proportion are auto personal injury cases; and businesses and insurers are heavy users of private ADR.

_____

[14]Survey, Question 22.

Chapter Four

THE PRODUCT: PRIVATE ADR PROCEDURES

The second major component of the private ADR marketplace is the product—the dispute resolution procedure. Private ADR's proponents argue that private ADR procedures are more flexible, quicker, less expensive, and more private than the public court option. Private ADR's opponents reply that these benefits are undocumented and do not necessarily outweigh the costs of growth in the new system—costs that may have grave public consequences.

In this chapter, we first describe the common types of ADR procedures that are available to consumers. Then, drawing on our firm interviews and firm caseload data and on our independent neutral survey responses, we determine what types of procedures are actually being offered in the Los Angeles marketplace, what types of procedures are being used, and what fee structures apply.[1] In this analysis, we consider the private ADR market as a whole and its components, firm and independent-neutral activity, separately. The measures we use are

- **Procedures offered**—The range of procedures offered by the private ADR providers is an important measure of the variety of private ADR available to meet the needs of disputants in the marketplace. If the range is broad, it indicates that variety is available in the market. If it is narrow, this alleged benefit of the private marketplace may not exist.

---

[1]Unfortunately, our data do not allow us to measure time to disposition.

- **Procedures provided**—The mix of procedures actually provided by the ADR providers is a measure of the extent to which the disputants are taking advantage of the available variety of the private ADR market. If a wide mix of procedures is actually being provided, disputants are taking advantage of the available variety; if a narrow mix of procedures is being provided, variety is not now an important benefit of private ADR.

- **Fees**—The fee structure of the industry provides an imperfect proxy of the costs of private ADR procedures. A high fee structure would suggest that the claim that private ADR is less expensive than litigation in the public courts bears further examination. However, this measure is only a partial proxy for the costs of private ADR procedures. Since attorneys' fees and costs account for most of the costs of dispute resolution in the public courts, this measure is in no way conclusive.

Privacy is often cited as another benefit of private ADR. We do not discuss it here beyond noting that it is fairly clear that, in comparison to dispute resolution in the public courts, private ADR offers procedural privacy and leads to more-private outcomes than are available in the public sector. There is no public exposure of information presented at the proceedings, and the decision has no precedential value. Of course, there is considerable debate over whether or not the privacy feature is a cost or a benefit of private ADR.

FORMS OF ADR PROCEDURE

It is helpful to begin with definitions of the various dispute resolution formats or procedures that might be offered by private providers. The taxonomy in private ADR is particularly confusing, since firms, neutrals, and disputants may use different terms to refer to the same procedure or concept. To clarify our use of these terms, we offer the following definitions:

- **Arbitration**—Arbitration is any adjudicatory procedure in which a neutral third party (or panel) hears arguments and reviews evidence provided by the disputants regarding the dispute between them. The neutral (or panel) then renders a final, binding decision, which is not subject to court approval or appeal.[2]

- **Mediation**—In mediation, disputants engage in discussions with each other through a third party in an attempt to reach a mutually agreed upon settlement of the dispute. This procedure operates under an entirely different paradigm from arbitration. Arbitration is based on the adjudicatory model of the public courts—passive fact-finding and binding procedure. Mediation, in contrast, is a nonbinding procedure in which the third-party neutral plays an active role in reaching a settlement of the dispute.

- **Private Judging**—"Private judging" refers to any procedure under Cal. Civ. Proc. Code §§ 638, 639 or Cal. Const., art. VI, § 21 in which the parties compensate the third-party neutral. Under this definition, a case first must be filed in court, after which, by agreement of the parties, on motion of one of the parties or on motion of the court, the entire action or some particular aspect of the action may go to private ADR procedure—typically an arbitration—for resolution. The decision reached in the private ADR procedure will be reported to the court and will be treated as the decision of the court, with all postjudgment remedies available including appeal.[3]

- **Summary Jury Trial**—A summary jury trial is a nonbinding procedure in which a private jury is empanelled from regular jury lists. The parties present short summaries of their cases. The jury then provides the parties with the realistic reactions of "real jurors." This nonbinding process provides parties with important information regarding the case for use in settlement.

- **Mini-Trial**—The mini-trial is another hybrid dispute resolution process which promotes negotiation and settlement. The par-

---

[2]This study specifically excludes court-annexed arbitration. Court-annexed arbitration is not a choice for disputants, because, in California, it is mandatory for all superior court cases in which the amount at issue is under $50,000. Decisions are also not binding. In addition, court-annexed procedures have been studied reasonably extensively. For a summary of these studies, see National Center for State Courts/State Justice Institute (1994).

[3]For a detailed study of this form of private ADR, see Roehl, Huitt, and Wong (1993).

ties' attorneys make short presentations to a third-party neutral sitting with high-level agents of the parties. After the presentations, the neutral offers his or her opinion to the parties. In addition, the parties' agents can ask questions of the neutral. Again, the purpose of this exercise is to provide the parties with information and an independent, nonbinding opinion of the dispute to promote settlement.

- **Voluntary Settlement Conference**—A voluntary settlement conference is very similar to a mediation or a court-mandated judicial settlement conference. However, the neutrals in mediation are expected to be much more assertive than neutrals in a voluntary settlement conference. In mediations, neutrals may offer opinions about the strengths and weaknesses of the various disputants' arguments and propose creative solutions. In voluntary settlement conferences, neutrals allow the disputants to direct the negotiation (see MacCoun et al., 1992).

- **Neutral Expert Fact-Finding**—Neutral expert fact-finding is a procedure in which certain substantively difficult or technical issues within a dispute are referred to an expert for determination. This procedure can be used by voluntary agreement of the parties or at the direction of the court. The determination made by the expert may be adopted by the court in which the dispute is being heard.

PROCEDURES OFFERED

Variety in ADR procedures offered by providers is an important measure of the flexibility available to consumers. Variety comes in three forms. Providers may offer a number of types of available procedures, for example, arbitration and mediation. For each procedure, considerable variation exists between the firms. Finally, the firms may also offer customers the opportunity to vary the rules applied within any type of procedure. This variation and the opportunities to tailor procedures are important measures of flexibility.

Procedural Options Among Firms

All the firms in our group advertise themselves as offering virtually all of the services described above.[4] Table 4.1 shows the availability of the various procedures offered by each ADR firm.

Within each type of procedure, variation is typical. For example, firms report offering several varieties of arbitration, such as high-low arbitration and mediation-arbitration.[5] Procedural rules can also vary. The arbitration rules of some firms make only rare reference to the Rules of Evidence, while others claim to apply the rules to their full extent. Similarly, the amount of prearbitration procedure varies considerably. Some rules allow parties the opportunity to obtain discovery and to have prearbitration procedures and motions heard. Under other rules, the parties cannot do either. The rules of mediation are as varied as the individuals who provide the service. Each has his or her own style and procedures. Some mediators only meet with disputants separately. Others also meet with the disputants together as they try to reach settlement. Some mediators want to know the substance of the dispute prior to the mediation session; others do not.

If formal options do not meet their needs, parties usually may create their own procedural flexibility by agreeing to alternative rules. The new rules may reflect an agreement regarding discovery or limiting the scope of the dispute, or they may address more substantive aspects of the dispute.

Procedural Options Among Independent Neutrals

Table 4.2 shows the percentage of independent neutrals who offer particular services. Comparing Table 4.2 to Table 4.1, we see that independent neutrals are less likely than firms to offer a broad range of procedural options to their clients. Ninety-eight percent of neutrals

---

[4]These claims of broad capability may be somewhat exaggerated in the interest of broad marketing.

[5]In high-low, the parties initially agree to low and high bounds for the value of the dispute. The arbitrator is then limited to this range in deciding the amount of the award. In mediation-arbitration the dispute is mediated, and any unresolved issues are then handled in an arbitration proceeding.

Table 4.1
Private ADR Firm Services

	Arbitration	Mediation	Private Judging	Mini-Trial	Summary Jury Trial	Expert Neutral Fact-Finding	Voluntary Settlement Conference	Mediation and Arbitration	Other
Alternative Resolution Centers	yes	yes	yes	yes	no	yes	yes[a]	no	no
American Arbitration Association	yes	yes	yes	yes	yes	yes	yes	no	no
Arbitration Forums, Inc.	yes	yes	yes	yes	yes	no	yes	no	no
Arts Arbitration & Mediation Service	yes	yes	no	no	no	no	yes[a]	no	no
First Mediation Corp.	yes	yes	yes	no	no	no	yes	yes	no
J.A.M.S., Inc.	yes	yes	yes	yes	yes	no	no	yes	no
Judicate, Inc.	yes	yes	yes	yes	yes	no	yes	yes	yes
Real Estate Mediation & Arbitration	yes	yes	no	yes	no	yes	yes	no	yes
United States Arbitration & Mediation	yes	yes	yes	yes	no	yes	no	no	no

SOURCE: Publicly available marketing information; firm interviews.

[a]Firm considers VSC to be mediation.

Table 4.2

Services Offered by Independent Neutrals
(percent)

Service	Percent
Arbitration	98
Mediation	55
Voluntary settlement conference	41
Expert neutral fact-finding	31
Private judging	28
Mini-trial	24
Discovery management	24
Summary jury trial	11
Other	8

SOURCE: Survey, Question 7.

in our survey report offering arbitration, while only 55 percent report offering mediation. Independent neutrals do offer other procedures, but less frequently than firms do. For example, seven of the nine firms in our survey offer mini-trials, while only 24 percent of the neutrals report that they offer this service. Although our survey did not address the question of flexibility within types of procedures, it is our impression that independent neutrals are less likely to formally codify or publish the rules they may use and that they are just as agreeable to variants that parties may agree to.

In sum, flexibility in both type of procedure offered and rules that apply is clearly available in the private marketplace.

Procedures Provided

The mix of services actually *provided* as opposed to the mix of procedures *offered* indicates the extent to which the flexibility of the private ADR market is being exploited by the disputants. If the disputants are not taking advantage of this flexibility, procedural variety may not be as valuable as many proponents argue. In this analysis, we categorize procedures provided as arbitration, mediation, private judging, voluntary settlement conferences, and other. The category "other" includes summary jury trials, med-arb, expert-neutral fact-finding, and mini-trials.

Procedures Provided by Firms

The mix of services actually provided through the firms is dominated by arbitration and mediation. Table 4.3 shows that arbitration accounts for 65 percent and mediation for an additional 24 percent of the services actually provided. All other services collectively account for only 11 percent of the disputes brought to private ADR firms.

Procedures Provided by Independent Neutrals

The independent neutrals provide a different mix of procedures to their clients (clients who come directly to them without going first to a firm), with arbitration and mediation playing a dominant but lesser role than in firms ($p < 0.01$). While arbitration accounts for 53 percent and mediation 21 percent of this caseload, voluntary settlement conferences account for 12 percent and private judging 7 percent of the procedures actually used. These latter figures compare with firm usage rates of 0.1 percent and 3 percent for voluntary settlement conferences and private judging, respectively.

Table 4.3

Mix of Services Actually Provided
(percentage of disputes)

Service	Firms[a]	Independent Neutrals[b]	Total Private ADR
Arbitration	65	53	58
Mediation	24	21	22
Private judging	3	7	5
Voluntary settlement conference	0[c]	12	7
Other	8	7	7

SOURCE: Firm data; Survey, Question 24.

NOTE: Percentages may not sum to 100 because of rounding.

[a]The firm data represent 1992 disputes.

[b]The independent neutral data represent 1993 disputes.

[c]The actual figure is 0.1 percent.

Total Private ADR Procedural Case Mix

Table 4.3 indicates that the private ADR market is dominated by arbitration (58 percent) and mediation (22 percent).[6] Seven percent were handled in voluntary settlement conferences and 5 percent in private judging.   The remaining 7 percent involve other mechanisms, including mini-trials, summary jury trials, and med-arb, which do not yet appear to be an important part of the private marketplace.[7]

Our findings demonstrate that, despite the opportunity that disputants may have to turn to new procedures for the resolution of their disputes, they tend to rely on the format that is most like the adjudicatory procedure of the courts: arbitration. At the same time, it is fair to characterize the procedural environment as one over which disputants have substantial control, if they choose to seek true alternatives to adjudication.

Trends

Although arbitration may currently dominate the marketplace, anecdotal information suggests that mediation and other ADR procedures are growing in popularity. Firms interviewed report that disputants are becoming more sophisticated in their understanding and use of ADR and are increasingly turning to mediation. This may be a reflection of the increasing sophistication of disputants, or it may be a consequence of growing familiarity with mediation as an alternative. In either case, the firms are marketing mediation services with growing energy.

Respondents to the survey of neutrals confirm that mediation is receiving a growing share of the private ADR market. When asked if they noticed a change in the mix of procedures they were providing, 60 percent of those who responded stated that they were mediating

---

[6]One large firm provider has recently added mediation to its available services and has not yet had significant usage of mediation. If this provider is eliminated from the market, the remaining firms show a mix of arbitration to mediation of 50 percent to 32 percent.

[7]The information provided by the individual providers regarding the frequency of usage of private judging conflicts with previous data; see Roehl, Huitt, and Wong (1993). This discrepancy warrants further research.

an increasing number of disputes; 13 percent stated that both mediation and arbitration were increasing; and 13 percent stated that other
forms of private ADR were growing in popularity.[8]

PRIVATE ADR FEES

One indicator of the comparative cost of private ADR is the fees
charged for private ADR services. This measure is of limited value,
because it omits attorneys' fees and costs, a large, and in some cases
overwhelming, part of the costs of dispute resolution.[9] Nonetheless,
since the fees charged for private ADR services can be large, and are
costs not associated with dispute resolution in the public courts, it is
important to understand them.

Fee structures vary depending upon whether disputes are being resolved through a firm or an independent neutral. Firms typically
charge administrative fees, hearing fees for their neutrals, and additional charges. Independent neutrals typically charge only an hourly
rate for their services. A small number of providers, both firms and
individuals, charge by the dispute, but this is rare.

Fee Structures for Firms

Administrative Fees. Table 4.4 shows that most private ADR firms
charge administrative fees that cover their management and other
business costs, and that these fees vary significantly across firms.
The typical fee is $100 to $150 per party for for-profit firms and from
none to a few thousand dollars for nonprofit firms.[10]

---

[8]Survey, Question 25.

[9]This very important information should be the subject of future research.

[10]The table and subsequent discussion rely on public information for the nine firms
serving the Los Angeles area that we originally characterized in Chapter Two (see pp.
11–12). As we noted above, several of these firms were not included in our data collection, because they were very small or handled a caseload that did not fall within the
scope of this study. Therefore, other parts of this report will refer to fewer firms than
we do here.

Table 4.4

Private ADR Firm Fees

Firm	Administrative Fee	Hourly Fee
Alternative Resolution Centers	$50/party	$250/hr (total for all parties)
American Arbitration Association	**Arbitration**—Sliding scale filing fee of $300 for cases under $25K, up to $4K for cases over $5M payable by filing party; plus an administrative fee of $100/day/party for 1 arbitrator, or $150/day/party for >1 arbitrator **Mediation**—$200 (cases under $100,000) or $300 (cases over $100,000) (total for all parties)	**Arbitration**—Based on arbitrator's fee, typically approximately $500/day/arbitrator **Mediation**—Based on mediator's fee
Arbitration Forums, Inc.	$150/party	Hourly, based on judge or attorney rate
Arts Arbitration & Mediation Service	**Arbitration**—Sliding scale based on income of party up to 4% of amount in controversy or $45/party **Mediation**—Small amount based on income of party	None
First Mediation Corp.	$100/party	2 parties $135/party/hr 3 parties $100/party/hr 4 parties $75/party/hr
J.A.M.S., Inc.	$100/party for 2-party dispute $125/party for 3 or more parties Some flat fee programs for cases under $50K $200–$450 (No hourly fee)	$150/hr/party if 2-party dispute; <$150/hr/party if more than 2 parties, determined by number of parties
Judicate, Inc.	**Business & Commercial—Arbitration & Mediation:** $300/party **Regular—Mediation:** $150/party	**Business & Commercial—Arbitration & Mediation:** $150/party/hr **Regular—Arbitration:** $300/party 1st hr, $150/party sub hrs **Mediation:** $450/party 1st hr, $150/party sub hrs

Table 4.4—continued

Firm	Administrative Fee	Hourly Fee
Real Estate Mediation & Arbitration	**Arbitration & Mediation—** $150/party	Hourly based on judge/ attorney rate
United States Arbitration & Mediation	$150/party if two-party dispute $100/party if more than two party dispute	**Arbitration—$250– 300/hr** **Mediation—$250/hr**
Public Court[a]	$15.00 small claims $80.00 municipal court $182.00 superior court	None

SOURCE: Publicly available information.

[a]Court data based on 1994 filing fees.

Administrative fees can be compared to filing fees in public courts, and they mirror court fees in that they generally take into account the value of the action and the number of parties. In the last row of Table 4.4, we have included the filing fees for the California state courts, which range between $15.00 and $182.00—or substantially below the fees charged by private ADR firms.

The biggest variation in administrative fees across firms is between the nonprofit and the for-profit firms. Nonprofit firms generally charge a fee based on either the size of the dispute or the income of the disputant. Administrative fees for the American Arbitration Association, for example, can be quite high if the amount at issue in the dispute is large. For-profit firms have slightly lower rates. However, since the costs of pursuing cases through for-profit firms generally entail higher hearing fees for the time of the neutral, differences in administrative costs may be overwhelmed by differences in hearing costs.[11]

Hearing Fees. Firms usually charge additional fees to cover the costs of the third-party neutral, and these fees vary substantially from firm to firm and within firms, depending on which neutral provides services. Table 4.4 reports the rates charged by the firms for which we have information. Fees fall in the range of $500/day-$450/hour. The

_____

[11]We did not systematically collect information on the lengths of hearings, but we understand that these lengths may vary substantially, with some approximating the time required by jury trials.

nonprofit firms in the group charge low or no hearing fees to cover the costs of neutrals, because neutrals usually serve on a voluntary or quasi-voluntary basis.   The for-profit firms range from $75/hour/ party to $450/hour/party.   In some cases, firms will also vary their hearing fees according to the amount at issue, the procedure used, and the number of parties in the action.   Rates typically do not vary between case types or disputant types.[12]

Other Fees. Parties may also be subject to additional fees, including transcript fees, reporters' costs, travel expenses, and conference room costs, if such services are requested or necessary.   In addition, most of the firms may impose cancellation fees, which can equal the cost of the neutral's time, if the procedure is not canceled prior to a certain date.   However, these fees are rarely imposed, so the total cost of the ADR service is usually represented by the administrative and hearing fees.

Fee Structure for Independent Neutrals

Independent neutrals typically charge only for the time they actually spend on the dispute, including research and travel time, as well as the actual hearing time.   In addition, disputants will typically be required to pay for any of the abovementioned additional costs.

Hourly fees vary considerably among independent neutrals, and two characteristics—whether or not they are affiliated with a firm panel and their professional background—explain much of the variation.

Table 4.5 shows the hourly fees for third-party neutrals reported by our survey respondents. The mean for the group is $208.96 per hour, while the median fee for all neutrals is $200.00 per hour. This difference reflects the skewed distribution of fees, with a few neutrals charging high fees. Looking at the fees by professional background (former judges, attorneys, and all others), we find that judges command the highest fee (median of $250.00 per hour) and those without formal legal training command the lowest (median of $150.00 per hour).

---

[12]Some firms note that they will work out fee arrangements that may vary from the scheduled rates for certain clients with a high amount of business.

Table 4.5

Median Hourly Fee by Background and Firm Affiliation
(dollars)

	Firm Affiliated	Non-Firm Affiliated	All Affiliations
Former judges	250	287	250
Attorneys	200	200	200
Non-attorneys	150	225	150
All providers	200	250	200

SOURCE: Survey, Question 32.

There is additional variation in rates between those neutrals who offer their services through firms and those who are not listed on the panels of any firms. Judges and "others" who provide services through the private ADR firms typically charge lower hourly fees than do the independent neutrals. For example, the median rate for judges affiliated with firm panels is $250 per hour, while it is $287 for judges who provide their services independent of firms. However, the median rate is the same for attorneys, whether or not they have firm affiliations.

The data show that fees do not systematically vary with other characteristics. While fees do increase somewhat with ADR experience, this increase is not systematic and may be less a reflection of growing expertise in ADR than an age bias; judges and attorneys who have had long histories of jurisprudence command high fees regardless of the length of time they have been providing private ADR. Likewise, there is no systematic relationship between the number of disputes heard and the fees commanded by a neutral.

In summary, our survey indicates that flexibility is available to the consumers of private ADR services. Currently, disputants opt for the private ADR procedure most like that offered by the courts: arbitration. Anecdotal information indicates that other forms of private ADR procedure, particularly mediation, are increasingly being used. Cost is difficult to compare, because many of the costs associated with resolving a dispute are attorneys' fees, and this information is not captured in this survey. Nonetheless, we observe that the fees for private ADR services do vary and usually greatly exceed those levied by the courts.

Chapter Five

SERVICE PROVIDERS: THIRD-PARTY NEUTRALS

The source and quality of third-party neutrals figure prominently in the debate over the potential costs and benefits of private ADR. Many engaged in the debate raise concerns that the private sector, with its opportunity for higher incomes and more hospitable working conditions, may lure good judicial talent from the public bench (see Reuben, 1994, and Galanter and Lande, 1992).

Critics also worry that disputants in private ADR may be receiving seriously flawed justice (see Reuben, 1994, and Galanter and Lande, 1992). Third-party neutrals who provide private ADR services are completely unregulated. Neither the state nor any broadly recognized professional group has developed a set of agreed-upon qualifications or licensing requirements to apply to this group.[1] Thus, the question of quality in private ADR remains. The issue is particularly compelling, because a number of state courts and the U.S. Supreme Court have strengthened the binding nature of arbitration, substantially narrowing the grounds for appeal. Furthermore, many are of the opinion that predispute contract agreements cast the "voluntary" nature of private ADR into question and that, particularly in disputes brought to private ADR because of a predispute contract, parties may be quite unequal in their ability to protect their own interests within its confines.

---

[1]The California Judicial Council has adopted a behavioral code to guide neutrals who hear court-referenced cases, but no code applies to all third-party neutrals ("California Adopts Rules Governing Private Judging," 1993). The question of what qualification and licensing requirements might be appropriate is currently a topic of intense debate in the profession. See, for example, SPIDR Commission on Qualifications (1993).

While this research does not provide us with the information necessary for directly assessing the validity of these concerns, our survey of
third-party neutrals provides data on important characteristics of
this population. A number of these characteristics might well be
linked with the ability of neutrals to provide appropriate and equitable services. These characteristics include

- **Sociodemographic Characteristics.**   While the sociodemographic characteristics of a particular individual (age, gender,
and ethnicity) shed little light on that individual's ability as a
neutral, diversity within the population of neutrals may be important in servicing a diverse set of disputants and disputes.

- **Training, Years in ADR, and Specialization.** In the absence of
more-direct measures of quality, a neutral's background—including legal training, experience on the bench, training in ADR
techniques and procedures, ADR experience, and substantive
expertise—is a useful proxy for his or her ability to perform in
this role.

In addition to determining these characteristics, our survey of neutrals allows us to link them with the number of cases handled in
1993, the type of case, the types of ADR services rendered, and claim
and award ranges.

In this chapter, we use these measures to report on the characteristics of the neutral population serving the Los Angeles area. We
examine the total population. We then turn our attention to the
small proportion that handles 100 or more cases per year and that
accounts for 59 percent of the total private caseload. Finally, we
examine the caseload characteristics of independent neutrals.

CHARACTERISTICS OF THIRD-PARTY NEUTRALS

Sociodemographic Characteristics

In addition to looking at sociodemographic characteristics of the
neutral community as a whole, we analyzed various subpopulations,
including those with different professional backgrounds and those
with and without firm panel affiliations. Table 5.1 presents the results of this analysis and contains few surprises. Neutrals, as a group,

Table 5.1

Sociodemographic Characteristics of Neutrals

	Percentage of Total	Age		Percentage Male	Ethnicity (percent)			
		Median	Mean		White	African-American	Latino	Other
All neutrals (N=1212)		60	58	94	95	2	2	2
By background[a]								
Lawyers (N=785)	67	54	55	95	95	2	2	2
Judges (N=91)	8	72	71	97	97	2	0	2
Other (N=301)	26	59	59	90	95	2	2	2
By panel[b]								
On firm panels (N=1013)	88	58	57	94	95	2	2	2
Not on firm panels (N=140)	12	62	60	94	97	1	1	1

SOURCE: Survey, Questions 1, 4, and 41–43.
[a]No answer for 35 neutrals.
[b]No answer for 59 neutrals.

come from the ranks of experienced professionals. Eight percent are former judges; 67 percent are attorneys; and the remaining 25 percent have a diverse set of other backgrounds. Their median age is 60 years, with some tendency toward clustering in the 40s and later 60s. Lawyers tend to be somewhat younger, while former judges tend to be somewhat older. The majority are listed on one or more firm panels.

There is very little diversity in the community of neutrals. Women are poorly represented, with fewer of them coming from the ranks of the judiciary and a relatively greater number from the category of "other." These results suggest that women without legal training may face fewer external barriers to entry and/or feel role boundaries somewhat less acutely. Representation from minority ethnicities is similarly low.

Characteristics Relating to Training and Experience

Table 5.2 shows that somewhat more than half of the neutral population has had some form of training or apprenticeship in ADR techniques, with neutrals who are former judges and neutrals who are not panel members substantially less likely to have had training. Much of this variation can be explained by firm practices. Most firms provide training sessions in ADR procedures and techniques for new panel members. The one large firm that does not provide training empanels only former judges. Independent neutrals who have had judicial experience are less likely, probably, to believe themselves in need of training, while those with no legal background are more likely to want the additional training.

The population of neutrals in Los Angeles has substantial dispute resolution experience. Judges, on average, tend to have been rendering ADR services for fewer years than others, because they tend to start somewhat later in their careers. And while the median years in ADR for all neutrals is eight, a few have been in the business substantially longer; several report over 30 years of experience. Although many judges enter the private sector with exactly 20 years of experience on the bench, there is a wide distribution in both directions around this number, with several reporting as little as four years and a few as many as 30 years. Twenty appears to be a marker year, because judges become eligible for retirement benefits after 20 years of

Table 5.2

Training and Experience of Neutrals

	Training		Years in ADR		Years on Bench (judges only)	
	Formal	Apprentice and Other	Median	Mean	Median	Mean
All neutrals (N=1212)	47	6	8	11	NA	NA
By background[a]						
Lawyers (N=785)	44	6	9	12	NA	NA
Judges (N=91)	21	10	6	7	20	19
Other (N=301)	63	8	7	9	NA	NA
By panel[b]						
On firm panels (N=1013)	49	7	8	11	20	18
Not on firm panels (N=140)	35	6	8	9	20	21

SOURCES: Survey, Questions 1, 2, 4, and 5.

[a]No answer for 35 neutrals.

[b]No answer for 59 neutrals.

service.[2] Judges are somewhat more likely to leave the bench prior to retirement if they join a firm's panel—a work setting in which they are likely to have a somewhat more assured stream of clients.

CHARACTERISTICS OF "HEAVY HITTERS"

The above description characterizes the total population of neutrals available to consumers in the marketplace, but is it a profile of the neutrals actually handling the private caseload? That is, how are disputes distributed across this population of neutrals, and if they are distributed unevenly, what are the characteristics of those neutrals providing the bulk of the services? Put another way, what characteristics do consumers seem to prefer? Figure 5.1 shows that more than half of all neutrals see fewer than 10 disputes annually, while less than 10 percent of the neutrals see more than half of the disputes.

---

[2]A judge qualifies to receive a pension equal to 65 or 75 percent of his or her salary at the time of retirement if the judge has satisfied age and term requirements (see Cal. Government Code §§ 75025, et seq. 1992).

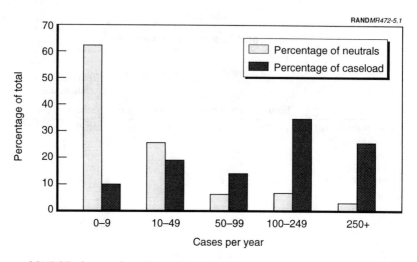

SOURCE: Survey, Question 13.

**Figure 5.1—Distribution of Number of Cases Across the
Neutral Population**

Since disputes are so highly concentrated in the hands of relatively few neutrals, we also looked at the characteristics of the 57 neutrals who each handled 100 or more disputes in 1993. Almost half of this group of neutrals (46 percent) come from the bench, while 49 percent are attorneys, and only 5 percent have other professional backgrounds. They are somewhat older as a group (median age 67 compared with 60 years), and a smaller percentage have had formal training in ADR (39 percent compared with 47 percent). But in other respects, the "heavy hitters" very much resemble the total population of neutrals.[3]

_____

[3]This statement reflects comparisons between the two groups along many dimensions, including case type, service provided, claim amount, award amount, and hourly fees.

NEUTRALS' CASELOAD CHARACTERISTICS

In addition to determining what sociodemographic, training, and experience   characteristics[4] typify the community of neutrals, we used information from the survey of neutrals to explore the relationship between the professional background of neutrals and the type of dispute, the size and value of their independent caseloads, and the types of procedures they typically use for these cases.[5] Because these disputes come directly to the neutrals, our results will not be confounded by the influence of a neutral's affiliation with a particular firm.

The professional background of neutrals has a substantial effect on the mix of disputes they handle. Tables 5.3a and 5.3b show that there is a significant difference (p < 0.01) among the types of cases handled by neutrals with different backgrounds. The case mix of former judges is dominated by auto personal injury disputes, while attorneys additionally handle a significant number of personal injury employment disputes.

Over half of all environmental, malpractice, non-auto personal injury, product liability, and real property cases are heard by former judges, while 88 percent of all employment and 58 percent of "other contract" disputes are heard by attorneys. Interestingly, although they represent only 8 percent of all neutrals, former judges are responsible for hearing 42 percent of all disputes.

Similarly, in Table 5.4, we see significant differences (p < 0.01) in the value of the caseloads of former judges, attorneys, and other neutrals. While attorneys handle almost 70 percent of all cases claiming less than $25,000, former judges handle over half the cases in each of the higher claim categories. These results are consistent with our observation above, that former judges handled a disproportionate share of certain types of cases, for example, malpractice, that may be above average in value. But, since auto personal injury is such a large fraction of the total caseload, these data suggest that former judges

---

[4]In Chapter Four, we also examine the relationship between professional background and fees.

[5]We have no comparable data for cases handled through firms.

Table 5.3a

Distribution of Case Types Within Provider Backgrounds (percent)

| Case Types | Provider Background | | | Total Case Type |
	Judge	Lawyer	Other	Distribution
Auto personal injury	47	46	42	46
Employment	2	26	20	16
Other contracts	8	10	7	9
Non-auto personal injury	10	3	9	6
Real property	8	4	3	5
Malpractice	9	1	2	5
Construction	5	4	4	4
Other tort	4	2	3	2
Other	3	2	5	2
Product liability	2	1	1	2
Consumer disputes	2	2	3	2
Environmental	1	0	0	1

SOURCE: Survey, Questions 1 and 26.
NOTE: Percentages may not sum to 100 because of rounding.

Table 5.3b

Distribution of Provider Backgrounds Within Case Types (percent)

| Case Types | Provider Background | | |
	Judge	Lawyer	Other
Auto personal injury	42	53	5
Employment	5	88	7
Other contracts	36	60	4
Non-auto personal injury	65	28	7
Real property	60	38	3
Malpractice	82	16	2
Construction	44	51	5
Other tort	59	34	6
Other	53	35	11
Product liability	62	34	3
Consumer disputes	45	48	8
Environmental	84	13	4
Total provider distribution	42	53	5

SOURCE: Survey, Questions 1 and 26.
NOTE: Percentages may not sum to 100 because of rounding.

Table 5.4

Distribution of Certain Types of Cases Coming to Neutrals by Professional Background[a]

Case Size ($ thousands)	Judge	Lawyer	Other	Percentage of Total Cases
<25	25	68	7	32
25–50	52	41	7	20
51–100	52	43	5	21
101–500	64	33	3	16
>500	63	32	5	11

SOURCE: Survey, Questions 1 and 29.
NOTE: Percentages may not sum to 100 because of rounding.
[a]Data for independent caseload only.

are more likely than attorneys to handle the more valuable cases of a given type, as well.

Finally, a neutral's professional background is likely to affect the type of procedure provided. Table 5.5 shows significant differences in services provided. In particular, former judges provide voluntary settlement conferences and "private judging" much more often than do attorneys, while attorneys provide arbitration to over two-thirds of their clients. These results strongly suggest that neutrals are chosen for and render the services that are the most familiar to them and about which they have the greatest knowledge.

Table 5.5

Procedures Provided by Neutral's Professional Background[a] (percent)

	Judges	Lawyers	Other	Total
Arbitration	38	69	34	53
Mediation	20	19	42	21
Voluntary settlement conference	22	4	11	12
Private Judging	14	2	1	7
Other	6	6	12	7

SOURCE: Survey, Questions 1 and 24.
NOTE: Percentages may not sum to 100 because of rounding.
[a]Data for independent caseload only.

In sum, our analysis of neutrals' characteristics indicates that they are not particularly diverse with respect to their sociodemographic characteristics. They are experienced professionals, and most have legal training and experience. Somewhat over 50 percent have had training in ADR practices and techniques, and the group as a whole has considerable experience delivering private ADR. Disputes are not divided evenly across the neutral population, and almost half the neutrals who handle over 100 cases per year are former judges. Otherwise, "heavy hitters" as a group have a profile that generally resembles neutrals as a whole. Finally, we learned that the professional background of neutrals influences their case mix and the procedures they are likely to provide.

Chapter Six

FINDINGS, DISCUSSION, AND FUTURE RESEARCH

At the outset of this report, we identified the major claims and allegations central to the current debate over the growth of private ADR, noting that the information to resolve them did not exist. The goal of this study is to develop the basic descriptive profile of the private ADR marketplace in Los Angeles, so that it might serve as the basis for more-focused inquiries into specific policy concerns. However, some of our findings do have direct or indirect bearing on these policy concerns. Therefore, in this chapter, we summarize our findings and discuss their implications for the current debate.

FINDINGS

The findings of this study of private ADR in Los Angeles bear on several sectors of the marketplace, including the caseload, the services provided within the private sector, and the characteristics of the service providers, the third-party neutrals. Our principal findings are summarized here.

Findings Regarding Caseload Characteristics

- **Size.** Although the private caseload is a small fraction of all formal disputes in Los Angeles, it is a rapidly growing fraction.

- **Dispute Characteristics.** The disputes going to private ADR are relatively high-value and durable disputes. Almost half are auto personal injury disputes.

- **Disputant Characteristics.** Both businesses and individuals are well represented in the disputant population in private ADR, and it appears that insurers play a very important role in bringing both types of disputants to the alternative forum.

Findings Regarding Private ADR Procedures

- **ADR Procedures Offered.** The private marketplace offers a full range of procedural options from which a consumer may choose. In addition, consumers usually may, by mutual agreement, tailor the rules of a procedure. Independent neutrals are less likely than firms to offer less-standard procedures—for example, minitrials or summary jury trials.

- **Use of Private ADR Procedures.** Although a wide variety of procedures is available, consumers show a strong preference for the more traditional forms of ADR—arbitration and, to a lesser degree, mediation. There is, however, some evidence of growing interest in other forms.

- **Fees Associated with Private ADR.** The fee structure for private arbitration is complex and variable. Firms charge administrative fees, hearing fees, and fees to cover other costs. Independent neutrals typically charge only an hourly rate for their time. These fees typically exceed fees imposed by courts during litigation.

Findings Regarding Third-Party Neutrals

- **Sociodemographic Characteristics.** Neutrals cover a broad age range, but are homogeneous with respect to gender and ethnicity.

- **Training and Experience.** Neutrals as a group have a broad base of legal training and ADR experience. Seventy-five percent have legal training, and 8 percent are former judges. In addition, more than half have some form of training in ADR procedures and techniques, and they average 11 years as providers of ADR services.

- **Characteristics of Heavy Hitters.** Most disputes are handled by a small share of neutrals. While 62 percent see fewer than 10 cases per year and account for only 9 percent of the total caseload, 8 percent of the neutrals see over 100 cases per year, accounting for 59 percent of the caseload. Almost half (46 percent) are former judges. Otherwise, this group of "heavy hitters" does not differ markedly from neutrals as a whole along the dimensions that we examined.

- **Professional Experience and Caseload Characteristics.** The professional experience of neutrals is likely to have implications for their case mixes and for the types of procedures they provide. Former judges are somewhat more likely to see certain types of less-common cases (for example malpractice and environmental disputes) and higher-value disputes. Attorneys are far more likely to arbitrate disputes than judges or "others," and judges are far more likely than attorneys or "others" to provide procedures that approximate those of the court.

DISCUSSION

While they do not directly address or resolve the issues surrounding private ADR, these findings are strongly suggestive of answers to several important points in controversy.

Effects of Private ADR on the Courts

Reducing the Court's Workload. At the moment, private ADR cannot be lightening the civil caseload of courts in Los Angeles to any appreciable degree. The private caseload is simply too small. However, our findings suggest that it does have considerable potential for accomplishing this goal eventually, because it is such a rapidly growing component of all dispute resolution activity. Furthermore, a disproportionate share of high-value and durable disputes—disputes that might be expected to consume larger-than-average amounts of court time— go to private ADR, suggesting it holds even greater potential for reducing the demands on the courts than might initially be expected.

Diverting Judicial Talent. The results of our study do not enable us to conclusively confirm or deny that the private sector is stripping the bench of valuable judicial talent. We can say that about 91 former judges are now offering their services in Los Angeles as neutrals in private ADR. Most of them retired from the bench following 20 years of service and therefore cannot be accused of leaving the bench "prematurely." On the other hand, it is likely that, absent the option of becoming a neutral, a number of them would not have chosen to retire but rather would have contributed some additional years of service on the bench. Thus, private ADR may well be "stripping the bench" of some judges, but at least thus far, it does not seem to be attracting them in substantial numbers before retirement age.

It remains to be decided at what point a move to the private sector ceases to be "stripping the bench" and becomes a desirable "transition" opportunity. It may be that the private sector offers senior judges an appropriate chance to work and then incrementally "wind down" their practices according to their own preferences or in response to signals from the marketplace—signals that are harder to send to sitting judges.

It is frequently asserted that the problem of "stripping" is not a problem of numbers but one of talent—that "the best talent" is going to the private sector. If this is, indeed, the case, it will lend more credence to concerns that the private sector will become a source of two-tiered justice serving the affluent. However, our study is unable to address this issue.

Impeding the Court's Ability to Establish Precedent and Reinforce Social Norms. Some opponents of private ADR argue that its growth will divert cases that may have precedential value and reduce the courts' ability to reinforce social standards through the public decision process. Characteristics of the current marketplace certainly do not justify these fears. Not only is the proportion of the total dispute caseload going to the private sector small, but auto personal injury disputes account for almost half of the private caseload. These are not characteristics that immediately suggest the public sector is losing important cases.

Opponents' concerns may be more nearly realized in the future, however, if *large proportions* (whether or not the actual numbers are large) of particular kinds of disputes over issues where the case law is still fluid are diverted to the private sector through predispute contracting; examples might be medical malpractice or environmental disputes.

Quality of the Private Sector

Assuring Procedural Quality. Private ADR differs from public adjudication in two ways that bear on quality. Neutrals are not selected on the basis of and held to any public standards. Furthermore, private proceedings are not public and therefore are not subject to the kind of scrutiny that may encourage neutrals to be attentive to quality.[1] Particularly because case law now makes appeal of any private ADR decision exceedingly difficult, there is good reason to focus on the issue of quality control in the private setting. Although we cannot draw any direct conclusions regarding the quality of the private ADR providers or services from the findings of our study, some of the results are certainly suggestive.

In general, it is fair to say that neutrals, as a group, have substantial training: They are likely to have legal training; they often have specific training (albeit probably not extensive) in ADR procedures and techniques; and they have been providing services for a number of years. Thus, to the degree that experience is a proxy for quality, Los Angeles neutrals, on average, should be competent. However, relying on "experience" as the source of quality may have its own problems, in that our findings indicate that the more closely coupled a neutral is with the adjudicative paradigm, the less likely he or she is to use alternatives to that paradigm. Thus, neutrals would seem to be unlikely catalysts for major procedural shifts. It is possible, on the other hand, that, in confining themselves to the more traditional procedural formats, neutrals are simply responding to the demands of the parties or the agents of the parties. If demand shifts, so will the menu of services they render.

Assuring Fairness of Outcome. Many argue that the impartiality essential to fair decisions cannot be counted on in the private sector, because financial incentives work to the contrary. This is the

---

[1]Few firms report having any formal quality-assurance mechanisms, although some actively solicit feedback from clients on their satisfaction with the services of the neutral(s).

"repeat-player problem." According to the logic of these critics, providers (firms and neutrals), because they want to retain the loyalty of valued customers, will favor those clients who are likely to bring repeat business. A number of our findings bear on this issue.

Our findings clearly indicate that private ADR is a *business* for the providers who account for most of the caseload. Even most nonprofit firms behave competitively as they tailor their offerings and seek new clients. For the neutrals who handle most of the private caseload, private ADR is a serious professional and economic endeavor, occupying much of their time. Both firms and the neutrals handling most of the disputes (although not necessarily most of the neutrals) can, therefore, be expected to be quite sensitive to the satisfaction of customers they value.

This said, one cannot automatically conclude that neutrals are likely to bias their decisions to please certain customers. It may well be that firms and neutrals see the best avenue to long-term success in establishing a clear reputation for fairness;[2] after all, both parties must agree to any choice of neutral, and even repeat customers may well prefer a fair neutral to one who may show bias.[3]

Preserving Access to Private ADR. In the past, ADR was the province of nonprofit firms and pro-bono neutrals. As such, it has been heralded as the solution for those who cannot afford the costs of disputing in the courts.[4] As private ADR becomes a for-profit enterprise, is may substantially reduce disputing options for the less advantaged. Our results show that the costs specifically associated with ADR proceedings are likely to be substantially higher than court costs. We do not, however, compare the total costs of public- and private-sector disputing, and it is this comparison that is most meaningful.

---

[2]See the comments of Judge Knight in Reuben (1994, p. 55).

[3]In addition, case law establishes that one of the few grounds for attacking an arbitrator's decision is bias. See Cal. Civ. Proc. Code §1286.2 (1992).

[4]It should be noted that while this argument is made, the data do not consistently support the proposition that ADR is cheaper than going to court. See Reuben (1994, p. 54).

FURTHER RESEARCH

To reaffirm the cautionary note we sounded at the beginning of this report, it is important to remember that, while our findings may be suggestive, they describe only one private ADR marketplace. Although we have no reason to believe that Los Angeles differs from what is now or what will be occurring shortly in other major metropolitan areas, legal cultures can differ markedly from place to place. Therefore, the next step must be to determine whether or not our findings apply in other locales. Beyond that step, this descriptive analysis lays the groundwork for important additional research.[5]

Consequences for Disputants

Although it is often argued that private dispute resolution offers significant practical benefits to disputants, there is little or no evidence verifying these benefits. To ascertain the value of this alternative form of dispute resolution, it would be useful to learn how total disputing costs (expert-witness fees, other case-development costs, and attorney fees) in the private sector compare with those in the public sector. Similarly, how do times to disposition vary between the two sectors, and how satisfied are disputants with the processes they encounter in private forums? Since it is unlikely that all types of disputes are equally well served by the same alternative procedure, it would also be helpful to know what kinds of disputes are most appropriate for the private forum and how cases and procedures might be productively matched.

At the same time, questions have been raised regarding the equity of outcomes in the private arena, and policymakers need to learn whether or not the market is structured in such a way that disputants of all stripes are likely to gain a fair and unbiased hearing. While concern regarding a potential bias favoring "repeat players" has focused on large businesses and insurers, attorneys are likely to be instrumental in selecting neutrals, and their role as repeat players should also be examined closely. In addition, the quality of the outcomes is likely to depend on the talents of the neutral, so a deeper

---

[5]For a similar but certainly not identical list, see Roehl (1994).

understanding of what particular talents lead to equitable and satisfying outcomes would be helpful.

Consequences for the Public Sector

While this study has presented some findings that suggest private ADR may well reduce the court workload, our results are far from definitive. To draw strong conclusions, we must know more about the characteristics of the disputes being resolved in private ADR. How complex are they? Would they have been litigated, and would they have settled early in the litigation process had they been pursued in the courts?

At the same time, private ADR may adversely affect the ability of the courts to attract and retain good judges. Our findings are both preliminary and mixed on this subject, and additional research is warranted.

Regarding the fear that the private sector may lay claim to important, precedent-setting disputes, we need to learn more about the types of cases and proportions of each type of case that are resolved through private ADR. It will be particularly important to examine how the use of predispute contracts is spreading and whether or not their spread might remove whole classes of disputes from the public sector. At the moment, this eventuality appears to pose private ADR's most significant threat to the evolution of case law.

Thus, while this study provides important information about the dynamics and characteristics of the private disputing marketplace, it leaves a number of questions unanswered. Because private ADR is likely to remain an important and growing phenomenon, these questions deserve further exploration.

A. DATA COLLECTION

The data we collected for this study consist of three separate information sets, each of which has different data identification and collection problems. In this appendix, we discuss these problems and
describe the choices we made. The three sets are Los Angeles County
Superior Court data, ADR firm data, and independent-neutral data.

LOS ANGELES COUNTY SUPERIOR COURT DATA

We use two sets of Los Angeles County Superior Court data. First, the
court maintains a case-level computerized data file of cases filed in
the *downtown branch* of the court. We obtained a magnetic tape
containing party names, type of action, filing and disposition dates,
and type of disposition for over 30,000 cases. However, this very extensive file has been of only marginal value to us because of its geo-
graphic limitation. Our study catchment area includes the entire Los
Angeles County, not just the downtown courthouse.

Second, the Judicial Council of California publishes an annual data
reference guide of aggregate caseload information for all California
courts. The Judicial Council asks all courts of appeal, superior
courts, and municipal courts to provide the number of filings and
resolutions in each court for both civil and criminal cases. In addition, the Council classifies cases brought in the superior court into
broadly defined types. The Annual Data References provide information on the basis of the courts' fiscal year, which runs from July 1
to June 30. For each calendar year reported in our study, we actually
use the fiscal year ending in that calendar year. For example, we use
the July 1, 1992 to June 30, 1993 information for our 1993 data.

ADR FIRM DATA

We collected two types of ADR firm data. First, we interviewed the nine firms that we identified as providing most of the private ADR services provided by firms in Los Angeles. Second, we attempted to gather case-level data from these firms.

Using telephone directories, professional directories, and professional publications, we developed a list of 22 firms that we thought provided ADR services. We screened these firms with a telephone interview and excluded the following from our sample: Los Angeles County Bar Association; Better Business Bureau; Center for Public Resources, Inc.; Association of Professional Arbitrators; California Motor Car Dealers Association; Center for Alternative Dispute Resolution; Court Arbitration Center; Hearsch Mediation Center; L. H. Joseph, Jr. and Associates, Inc.; Mediation Project, Inc.; Steven R. Sauer & Associates; and Scott Mediation. Most are, in reality, individual providers of services. Others provide services for no charge or simply refer disputants who contact them to independent neutral providers and do not charge for their services or keep any records of the disputants who contact them. These types of firms are outside the scope of our study. After eliminating them, nine firms remained that met our criteria.

We interviewed an individual at each of the nine firms who could provide detailed information concerning the disputants, caseload, and business of the firm's Los Angeles office. (In most cases, it was the firm's only office.) We used an open-ended interview instrument to obtain information comparable to what we expected to obtain from the courts and the independent neutrals. All nine firms cooperated in this phase of our data-collection effort, but we concluded that only six of the nine firms we interviewed actually provide services in Los Angeles County that met our definition of private ADR. Thus, our ultimate sample of firms is six.

In addition to the interview information, we attempted to obtain case-level data about the disputes from each of these six firms. We had anticipated that each firm would keep case-level data in computer or hard-copy case files, but two of the firms reported that they did not keep such data, and a third was unwilling to give us access to theirs. We were, however, able to gather case-level information from the remaining three firms. Two of them provided us with computer files for cases handled in 1993, and the third gave us access to their hard-copy case files, from which we abstracted information for all 1992 cases. Finally, one of the firms that reported it did not keep case-level data did share detailed aggregate information on its caseload. Thus, we collected caseload information from four firms.

INDEPENDENT-NEUTRAL DATA

The data collection for independent neutrals who provide private ADR services in Los Angeles County consisted of a mail survey with telephone follow-up. (A copy of the survey can be found in Appendix B.) We used three sources to locate independent neutrals. First, we reviewed all general and professional directories that list arbitrators, mediators, or private judges. These sources included telephone directories, the Directory of California Lawyers, Parker's Directory, and the Profiles of Retired Judges. Second, we reviewed professional periodicals and journals for advertisements and announcements. Last, we obtained the names of all neutrals used by the various private ADR firms we had identified.

The neutrals we identified fell into three groups, each requiring separate treatment. One ADR firm listed about 1,200 neutrals on its panel. Because we did not have the resources to survey every member of this list, we randomly sampled two persons in every seven from the list.[1] Another firm did not give us access to its panel members until after we had fielded the survey. Therefore, we surveyed this group of 25 neutrals using a shortened version of the instrument and received responses from 16. We sent surveys to *all* other providers not affiliated with the two above-mentioned firms. Each completed survey was then assigned a weight based on the non-response rate within the group its respondent came from and the sampling scheme for that group. All responses we report are weighted, based on our estimate of 1,212 neutrals serving Los Angeles.

---

[1] As noted in the report, this firm lists its entire membership as panel members, although a substantial number do not provide ADR services.

The survey process consisted of an initial mailing, a reminder mailing to nonrespondents one week after the initial mailing, a secondary mailing to nonrespondents one week after the reminder mailing, and a three-week telephone follow-up period, which began one week after the secondary mailing. The telephone questionnaire is a shortened version of the mail questionnaire.

Questionnaires were mailed to 715 potential respondents. Of these, 174 neutrals were identified as "ineligible"; they either had not provided private ADR in the past five years and were not actively promoting themselves as private ADR providers or were deceased.[2] Of the remaining 541 neutrals, 411 neutrals completed the survey, with 260 completing the mail survey and 151 completing the phone survey, for a total response rate of 76 percent.

To check the quality and reliability of our survey data, we did several things. First, we compared seven variables for telephone and mail respondents to determine if the type of survey might suggest any particular biases. The variables we examined were age, years of experience in ADR, background, panel membership, number of 1993 cases by source, award amount, and hourly fees. We performed t-tests and chi-square tests and found that there was no difference between mail and telephone survey responses for six of the variables tested (p-values ranged from 0.07 to 0.77). We concluded that the type of survey did not lead to any bias in our data and did not suggest any bias between respondents and nonrespondents.

Second, we were concerned with response error, since a considerable amount of the information we requested relied on recollection. Therefore, we checked certain responses for internal consistency and outliers. These variables included the number of direct 1993 cases by source (Question 13), time of referral (Question 18), service provided (Question 24), case type (Question 26), claim amount (Question 29), and award amount (Question 30). If an inconsistency of 50 or more disputes was found, we contacted the respondent to investigate the disparity. We also contacted the respondent if any individual response was grossly inconsistent with the other responses.

---

[2]The high ineligibility rate largely reflects the proportion of listed panel members in one firm who do not, in fact, provide neutral services.

We also compared the respondents' estimates of the number of cases referred to them by specific firms with the caseload estimates given us by those firms in interviews and/or the firm's case-level data. For example, we summed the independent-neutral responses for the number of disputes referred to them by Firm X, and compared the sum to the actual number of cases handled by Firm X according to Firm X's records. We found excellent consistency between the independent neutrals' responses and the actual firm data.

In one set of questions, it became clear that respondents misinterpreted the questions, but in a consistent manner. We, therefore, adjusted our analysis to accommodate their interpretation. The survey asked respondents to answer a number of questions specifically regarding disputes in their caseloads that could have been filed in Superior Court. We requested information on this subpopulation, because we hoped to compare the private ADR disputes with detailed case information obtained from the Superior Court. However, after reviewing the responses, it was apparent that the respondents did not limit their responses to these particular cases. For example, when asked about claim amounts for these cases, they reported that 31 percent of their cases claimed less than $25,000—or below the minimum for Superior Court. Similarly, if respondents had limited their disputes in some way, we should have observed more cases in the source variable (Question 13) than in the service, case type, claim amount, and award amount variables. Instead, as indicated previously, the answers are consistent across all these variables. Because respondents did not report on this subpopulation of disputes, we were not able to make as many private versus public comparisons with the Superior Court caseload as we had hoped.

B. SURVEY INSTRUMENT

Revised: 8/4/93

```
┌─────────────────────────────┐
│                             │
│      Bar Code ID Label      │
│                             │
└─────────────────────────────┘
```

Survey of Alternative Dispute Resolution Services

RAND
1700 Main Street
PO Box 2138
Santa Monica CA 90407-2138

IMPORTANT INSTRUCTIONS - PLEASE READ FIRST

• *Because we have selected a limited number of providers of ADR services, your participation is critical to the success of this research. The questionnaire is not as long as it looks, and you will find that it can be completed fairly quickly.*

• Specifically, we ask for information about your ADR caseload during January - July 1993. Please take a few minutes to locate calendars, diaries, logs, or any other available source to provide information.

• If you have not provided ADR services in 1993, this survey still applies to you.

• To answer the questions, please fill in your response on the line provided or place an 'X' in the box next to the response you choose. You should provide some information at each item, unless an instruction directs you to skip to a specific question.

• If you have any questions about a specific item, your participation, or the study in general, please call Erik Moller, Co-investigator, at RAND -- (310) 393-0411, ext. 6573.

1

A. General Information

We're interested in your background and experience providing <u>private ADR services.</u>

1. Are you a:

   (Check One Box)

   ☐ ₁ Non-lawyer mediator or arbitrator

   ☐ ₂ Lawyer

   ☐ ₃ Retired judge ⇒ Years on bench:_____

   ☐ ₄ Something else ⇒ Describe:_____

2. In what month and year did you first begin providing private ADR services? (Remember, we are interested only in private ADR, not court-annexed arbitration.)

   _____ Month   _____ Year

3. Do you have other employment in addition to your work in private ADR?

   (Check One Box)

   ☐ ₁ No

   ☐ ₂ Yes ⇒ Please describe:_____

4. Are you currently a member of any ADR provider panels? (For example, JAMS, ARC, AAA, or the Bar Association Panel.)

   (Check One Box)

   ☐ ₁ No

   ☐ ₂ Yes ⇒ List Firms:_____

   _____

   _____

   _____

5. Have you had training in arbitration, mediation, or other ADR techniques?

   (Check All That Apply)

   ☐ ₁ No formal training

   ☐ ₂ Formal training program; specify name: _____

   ☐ ₃ Informal apprenticeship

   ☐ ₄ Other, specify: _____

2

6.   Have you ever served as an arbitrator for court-annexed arbitration cases?
        (Check One Box)

        ☐₁ No

        ☐₂ Yes ⇒ Approx. # of Cases to Date:_____

7.   What types of ADR services do you <u>offer</u>?
        (Check All That Apply)

        ☐₁ Arbitration

        ☐₂ Mediation

        ☐₃ Private judging

        ☐₄ Mini-trial

        ☐₅ Summary jury trial

        ☐₆ Fact Finding

        ☐₇ Discovery Management

        ☐₈ Voluntary Settlement Conference

        ☐₉ Other, specify: _____

8.   Which of these services have you <u>provided</u>?
        (Check All That Apply)

        ☐₁ Arbitration

        ☐₂ Mediation

        ☐₃ Private judging

        ☐₄ Mini-trial

        ☐₅ Summary jury trial

        ☐₆ Fact Finding

        ☐₇ Discovery Management

        ☐₈ Voluntary Settlement Conference

        ☐₉ Other, specify: _____

9.   Do you specialize in any particular type of ADR services?
        (Check One Box)

        ☐₁ No

        ☐₂ Yes ⇒ Which ones?_____

              Why? _____

3

10. Do you specialize in any particular type of disputes?

    (Check One Box)

    ☐ ₁ No

    ☐ ₂ Yes ⇒ Which ones?_____

                Why?_____

11. Please estimate the total number of private ADR cases you handled for the years 1988-1992.

Est.1992 Total	Est.1991 Total	Est.1990 Total	Est.1989 Total	Est.1988 Total
_____	_____	_____	_____	_____

12. Have you provided any private ADR services for civil disputes in 1993? (Remember, we are interested only in private ADR services, not court-annexed arbitration.)

    (Check One Box)

    ☐ ₁ No ⇒ Skip to Section C, page 8

    ☐ ₂ Yes

B.   Alternative Dispute Resolution Services

These next few questions ask for general information about your **1993** private, civil caseload. We are interested in referral patterns for private ADR disputes in Los Angeles. Please answer questions 13-16 for all civil disputes you handled -- excluding family or probate disputes -- during January - July 1993.

13. How many private, civil disputes came to you in 1993 from each of the following sources? Please refer to any calendars, logs, diaries or other records you may have. *If you are unable to provide an actual count from your records, please provide your best estimate of the actual count.*

Referral Source	1993 Cases
ADR Organizations:	
AAA	_____
Arbitration Forums	_____
ARC	_____
Arts Arbitration & Mediation	_____
Equilaw	_____
First Mediation	_____
JAMS	_____
Judicate	_____
Real Estate Arbitration & Mediation	_____
U.S. Arbitration & Mediation	_____

4

13.   Continued.

Referral Source   1993 Cases

Other firms, (specify):

_____   _____
_____   _____
_____   _____
_____   _____

Direct Client Contact   _____

Bar Association (JASOP, etc.)   _____

Other (specify):

_____   _____

14.   Is this pattern of referral sources different than in previous years?

(Check One Box)

☐₁ No

☐₂ Yes ⇒ How?_____

_____

15.   In how many of your 1993 private ADR disputes was the amount in dispute more than $25,000? *If you are unable to provide an actual count from your records, please provide your best estimate of the actual count.*

Cases _____

16.   How many of your 1993 private ADR disputes could not have been pursued in Superior Court, either because the amount claimed fell below the $25,000 threshold or for jurisdictional reasons? *If you are unable to provide an actual count from your records, please provide your best estimate of the actual count.*

Cases _____

17.   Were all of your 1993 private ADR disputes referred to you by an ADR organization like JAMS, AAA, ARC, etc.?

(Check One Box)

☐₁ No

☐₂ Yes ⇒ Skip to Section C, page 8

5

We'd like some information on the cases that came to you directly during January - July 1993 including cases which came to you from Bar Association Referral (i.e. JASOP), but excluding cases that came to you through an organization like AAA, JAMS, Judicate, First Mediation, etc.

Please refer to calendars, logs, diaries or any other available records covering January - July of this year. *If you are unable to provide an actual count from your records, please provide your best estimate of the actual count.*

18.   Of the cases that came to you directly, how many came to you:

After filing, but
Before Superior Court filing:_____   early in the litigation:_____   Late in the litigation:_____

19.   Is this pattern different than in previous years? For example, are more cases coming to you before filing?

(Check One Box)

☐₁ No

☐₂ Yes ⇒ Describe:_____

_____

20.   How many of the cases that came to you directly in 1993 fall into each of the party profiles listed below?

Individual v. Individual: _____   # Business v. Individual: _____

Individual v. Business: _____   # Business v. Business: _____

21.   Is this pattern different than in previous years?

(Check One Box)

☐₁ No

☐₂ Yes ⇒ Describe:_____

_____

22.   In how many of the cases that came to you directly were disputants represented by, or had an attorney provided by, an insurance company?

Cases_____

23.   Compared to past years, does this reflect an:

(Check One Box)

☐₁ Increase   ☐₂ Decrease   ☐₃ No Change

6

24. How often did you provide each of the following types of ADR in 1993? Remember to limit your response to cases that came to you directly or through Bar Association Referral (i.e. JASOP) (not through an ADR organization) and that could have been pursued in Superior Court. *If you are unable to provide an actual count from your records, please provide your best estimate of the actual count.*

Service	1993 Cases
Arbitration (Excluding matters referred pursuant to Cal. Civ. Proc. Code Sections 638 & 639)	_____
Mediation	_____
Private judging (Matters referred pursuant to Cal. Civ. Proc. Code Sections 638 & 639)	_____
Mini-trial	_____
Summary jury trial	_____
Expert neutral fact finding	_____
Voluntary Settlement Conference	
Other, (specify):	
_____	_____
_____	_____
_____	_____
_____	_____

25. Is this pattern of services provided different than in previous years? For example, are you now conducting more mediation? Less arbitration?

(Check One Box)

☐ 1   No

☐ 2   Yes ⇒ Describe:_____

_____

7

26. In 1993, has your caseload included any of the types of disputes listed below. We know that a dispute will often involve more than one of these categories. However, please count each case only once and put it in the category that best describes it. [Remember to limit your response to cases that came to you directly or through Bar Association Referral (i.e. JASOP) and that could have been pursued in Superior Court.] *If you are unable to provide an actual count from your records, please provide your best estimate of the actual count.*

Subject Matter			# of Cases
BREACH OF CONTRACT:			
Real property	☐₁ No	☐₂ Yes ⇒	_____
Consumer disputes	☐₁ No	☐₂ Yes ⇒	_____
Other contracts	☐₁ No	☐₂ Yes ⇒	_____
TORT:			
Auto PI	☐₁ No	☐₂ Yes ⇒	_____
Other PI	☐₁ No	☐₂ Yes ⇒	_____
Medical malpractice	☐₁ No	☐₂ Yes ⇒	_____
Other malpractice	☐₁ No	☐₂ Yes ⇒	_____
Product Liability	☐₁ No	☐₂ Yes ⇒	_____
Other tort	☐₁ No	☐₂ Yes ⇒	_____
CONSTRUCTION:	☐₁ No	☐₂ Yes ⇒	_____
EMPLOYMENT/LABOR:	☐₁ No	☐₂ Yes ⇒	_____
ENVIRONMENTAL:	☐₁ No	☐₂ Yes ⇒	_____
OTHER:	☐₁ No	☐₂ Yes ⇒	_____

27. Is this case mix different than in previous years? For example, are you handling more of one type of dispute and less of another than you did before?

    (Check One Box)

    ☐₁ No

    ☐₂ Yes ⇒ Describe:_____

    _____

28. Of the cases that came to you directly in 1993, how many settled, were withdrawn, or did not otherwise complete the dispute resolution procedure (arbitration, mediation, etc.)? *If you are unable to provide an actual count from your records, please provide your best estimate of the actual count.*

        # Cases _____

8

29. Of the cases that came to you directly, how often did the amount asserted to be at issue at the inception of the case fall into the categories listed below? [Remember to limit your response to cases that came to you directly or through Bar Association Referral (i.e. JASOP) and that could have been pursued in Superior Court. *If you are unable to provide an actual count from your records, please provide your best estimate of the actual count.]*

Claim Amount	1993 Cases
Under $25,000	_____
$25,000 - 50,000	_____
$51,000 - 100,000	_____
$101,000 - 500,000	_____
Over $500,000	_____

30. How many <u>awards</u> from the 1993 cases that came to you directly fall into the categories listed below? (Remember to limit your response to cases that came to you directly or through Bar Association Referral (i.e. JASOP) and that could have been pursued in Superior Court. *If you are unable to provide an actual count from your records, please provide your best estimate of the actual count.)*

Award Amount	1993 Cases
Defense Verdict ($0)	_____
Under $25,000	_____
$25,000 - 50,000	_____
$51,000 - 100,000	_____
$101,000 - 500,000	_____
Over $500,000	_____

31. In recent years, has the average value of the disputes you handle:

    (Check One Box)

    ☐₁ Increased   ☐₂ Decreased   ☐₃ Stayed the same

C. **Your Fee Structure**

32. How do you bill clients?

    (Check All That Apply)

    ☐₁ Per hour ⇒ Amount:_____
    ☐₂ Per dispute ⇒ Amount:_____
    ☐₃ Pro bono
    ☐₄ Other ⇒ Describe:_____

9

33. Do your fees vary in any way?

    (Check One Box)

    ☐ 1 No

    ☐ 2 Yes ⇒ How? _____

                      _____

34. In addition to your fee, do clients pay additional fees or expenses such as facility rental, administration/filing fees, correspondence, or staff assistance fees?

    (Check One Box)

    ☐ 1 No

    ☐ 2 Yes ⇒ Describe:_____

35. Typically, who is responsible for payment?

    (Check One Box)

    ☐ 1 Equal responsibility among parties

    ☐ 2 Party initiating ADR

    ☐ 3 Party appointing ADR provider

    ☐ 4 Other, specify: _____

D. Promoting Use of ADR

36. We are interested in how the use of ADR is promoted. What type of outreach or marketing techniques do you rely on? (Be assured that all information you provide will be treated privately and confidentially.)

    (Check All That Apply)

    ☐ 1 Advertising ⇒ What publication(s): _____

    ☐ 2 Bar Association Referral (JASOP)

    ☐ 3 Court-annexed arbitration

    ☐ 4 Repeat clients

    ☐ 5 Educational forums or workshops

    ☐ 6 Consulting on ADR

    ☐ 7 Reputation or word of mouth

    ☐ 8 Other, specify:_____

10

E.   Your Perception of ADR

37.   What do you see as the <u>chief incentives</u> for businesses to use ADR?

_____

_____

38.   What do you see as the <u>chief barriers</u> for businesses to use ADR?

_____

_____

39.   What do you see as the <u>chief incentives</u> for individuals to use ADR?

_____

_____

40.   What do you see as the <u>chief barriers</u> for individuals to use ADR?

_____

_____

F.   We need the following socio-demographic information for statistical purposes.

41.   What is your age?

_____ Years

42.   Are you:

(Check One Box)

☐₁   Male

☐₂   Female

11

43.   Which category below best describes you?

(Check One Box)

☐ 1   White

☐ 2   African-American

☐ 3   Hispanic

☐ 4   Asian or Pacific Islander

☐ 5   Native American

☐ 6   Other, specify: _____

44.   What is your educational background?

(Check All That Apply)

☐ 1   B.A., B.S.

☐ 2   M.A., M.S.

☐ 3   Ph.D.

☐ 4   J.D.

☐ 5   L.L.D.

☐ 6   Other, specify: _____

If you have any rules that you apply generally to any or all of your ADR procedures, please include a copy of theses rules with your completed survey.

We may want to contact you to follow-up on the information you have provided or to ask additional questions. If you are willing to assist us by providing additional information, please write your daytime phone number below.

Daytime Phone Number: (_____) _____ - _____

Thank you for your cooperation. Please place your completed survey and any additional materials in the envelope provided.

RAND
1700 Main Street
PO Box 2138
Santa Monica CA 90407-2138

BIBLIOGRAPHY

Bryant, D., *Judicial Arbitration in California: An Update*, Santa Monica, Calif.: RAND, N-2909-ICJ, 1989.

"California Adopts Rules Governing Private Judging," *World Arbitration and Mediation Report*, Vol. 4, No. 3, 1993, p. 58.

Cooter, R., and D. Rubinfeld, "Economic Analysis of Legal Disputes and Their Resolutions," *Journal of Economic Literature*, Vol. 27, No. 3, 1989, pp. 1067–1097.

"Courts Must Ensure 'Fair' Cost Allocation in Referrals to Private Referees," *World Arbitration and Mediation Report*, Vol. 5, No. 3, March 1994, p. 60.

D'Amico, S., P. Friedman, M. Oram, and H. Schmidt, *California Judicial Retirement Study*, San Francisco: National Center for State Courts, 1988.

Dewey, K., "A White Knight to ADR's Reserve," *California Law Business*, September 13, 1993, p. 16.

"Dispute Resolution Clauses: A Guide for Drafters of Business Agreements," *Alternatives*, Vol. 12, No. 5, May 1994, pp. 66–71.

Donovan, K., "Searching for ADR Stars," *The National Law Journal*, March 14, 1994, p. A1.

"Exploring the Issues in Private Judging," *Judicature*, Vol. 77, No. 4, 1994, p. 203.

Flaherty, D., "ADR Industry: Rapid Growth Brings Pains," *Alternatives*, Vol. 11, No. 10, 1993, p. 133.

Galanter, M., and J. Lande, "Private Courts and Public Authority," *Studies in Law, Politics, and Society*, Vol. 14, 1992, pp. 393–415.

Garth, B., "Privatization and the New Market for Disputes: A Framework for Analysis and a Preliminary Assessment," *Studies in Law, Politics, and Society*, Vol. 12, 1992, pp. 367–391.

Goldberg, S., E. Green, and F. Sander, *Dispute Resolution*, Boston: Little, Brown and Company, 1985.

Hensler, D., A. Lipson, and E. Rolph, *Judicial Arbitration in California: The First Year*, Santa Monica, Calif.: RAND, R-2733-ICJ, 1981.

Howard, W., "The Evolution of Contractually Mandated Arbitration," *Arbitration Journal*, Vol. 48, No. 3, 1993, pp. 27–38.

Judicial Council of California, Annual Data Reference: 1991–93 Caseload Data by Individual Courts, 1994.

Judicial Council of California, Annual Data Reference: 1991–92 Caseload Data by Individual Courts, 1993.

Judicial Council of California, Annual Data Reference: 1990–91 Caseload Data by Individual Courts, 1992.

Judicial Council of California, Annual Data Reference: 1989–90 Caseload Data by Individual Courts, 1991.

Judicial Council of California, Annual Data Reference: 1988–89 Caseload Data by Individual Courts, 1990.

Judicial Council of California, Annual Data Reference: 1987–88 Caseload Data by Individual Courts, 1989.

Kakalik, J. S., M. Selvin, and N. M. Pace, *Averting Gridlock: Strategies for Reducing Civil Delay in the Los Angeles Superior Court*, Santa Monica, Calif.: RAND, R-3762-ICJ, 1990.

Kaplow, L., "Private versus Social Costs of Bringing Suit," *Journal of Legal Studies*, Vol. 15, No. 2, 1986, pp. 371–386.

Landes, W., and R. Posner, "Adjudication as a Private Good," *Journal of Legal Studies*, Vol. 8, No. 2, 1979, pp. 235–384.

MacCoun, R., E. Lind, and T. Tyler, *Alternative Dispute Resolution in Trial and Appellate Courts*, Santa Monica, Calif.: RAND, RP-117, 1992.

Moller, E., and E. Rolph, *Private Dispute Resolution in the Banking Industry*, Santa Monica, Calif.: RAND, MR-259-ICJ, 1993.

National Center for State Courts/State Justice Institute, "A Report on Current Findings—Implications for Courts and Future Research Needs," National Symposium on Court-Connected Dispute Resolution Research, 1994.

"Navigating the 90s," *The American Lawyer*, February 1994, supp. pp. 41–50.

Provine, D., "Justice a la Carte: On the Privatization of Dispute Resolution," *Studies in Law, Politics and Society*, Vol. 12, 1992, pp. 345–366.

Reuben, R., "The Dark Side of ADR," *California Lawyer*, February 1994, pp. 53–58.

Rocca, R., and J. Wong, "Clients Facing Many Format Choices," *California Law Business*, Los Angeles: The Los Angeles Daily Journal, September 13, 1993, p. 21.

Roehl, J., R. E. Huitt, and H. Wong, *Private Judging: A Study of Its Volume, Nature, and Impact on State Courts*, Pacific Grove, Calif.: Institute for Social Analysis, 1993.

Ross, R., *Government and the Private Sector: Who Should Do What*, New York: Crane Russak & Co., 1988.

Savas, E. S., *Privatizing the Public Sector*, Chatham, N.J.: Chatham House Publishers, Inc., 1982.

Shavell, S., "The Social versus Private Incentives to Bring Suit in a Costly Legal System," *Journal of Legal Studies*, Vol. 11, No. 2, 1982, pp. 333–340.

SPIDR Commission on Qualifications, *Qualifying Neutrals: The Basic Principles*, Society for Professionals in Dispute Resolution, 1993.

Stevenson, M., "Court Examines Growing Use of Private Judges," Los Angeles: *The Los Angeles Daily Journal*, March 17, 1994, p. A1.

Wilkinson, J., ed., *Donovan, Leisure, Newton, and Irvine ADR Practice Book*, New York: John Wiley & Sons, 1990.

Wolf, C., Jr., *Markets or Governments: Choosing Between Imperfect Alternatives*, Cambridge, Mass.: MIT Press, 1993.

9 U.S.C. § 1, *et seq.* (1988 & Supp. 1991).

Cal. Civ. Proc. Code §§ 1141.10, *et seq.* (1992).

Cal. Civ. Proc. Code § 1286.2 (1994).

Cal. Civ. Proc. Code § 1281 (1994).

Cal. Gov't. Code §§ 75025, *et seq.* (1992).

Burchell v. March, 58 U.S. 344, 349–350 (1854).

Gilmer v. Interstate/Johnson Lane Corp., 500 U.S. 20, 111 S. Ct. 1647 (1991).

Mitsubishi Motors Co. v. Soler Chrysler-Plymouth, Inc., 473 U.S. 614 (1984).

Moncharsh v. Heily & Blase, 3 Cal. 4th 1 (1992).

New York Arbitration Act, N.Y. Civ. Prac. L. & R. 7501–7514 (1980 & Supp. 1986).

Sherck v. Alberto-Culver Co., 417 U.S. 506 (1974).

United Steelworkers v. American Mfg., 363 U.S. 564 (1960).

United Steelworkers v. Enterprise Wheel & Car Co., 363 U.S. 583 (1960).

United Steelworkers v. Warrior & Gulf Nav. Co., 363 U.S. 574 (1960).

OUTCOMES

General

Carroll, S. J., with N. M. Pace, *Assessing the Effects of Tort Reforms*, R-3554-ICJ, 1987.

Galanter, M., B. Garth, D. Hensler, and F. K. Zemans, *How to Improve Civil Justice Policy*, RP-282. (Reprinted from *Judicature*, Vol. 77, No. 4, January/February 1994.)

Hensler, D. R., *Trends in California Tort Liability Litigation*, P-7287-ICJ, 1987. (Testimony before the Select Committee on Insurance, California State Assembly, October 1987.)

_____ , *Researching Civil Justice: Problems and Pitfalls*, P-7604-ICJ, 1988. (Reprinted from *Law and Contemporary Problems*, Vol. 51, No. 3, Summer 1988.)

_____ , *Reading the Tort Litigation Tea Leaves: What's Going on in the Civil Liability System?* RP-226. (Reprinted from *The Justice System Journal*, Vol. 16, No. 2, 1993.)

Hensler, D. R., M. E. Vaiana, J. S. Kakalik, and M. A. Peterson, *Trends in Tort Litigation: The Story Behind the Statistics*, R-3583-ICJ, 1987.

Hill, P. T., and D. L. Madey, *Educational Policymaking Through the Civil Justice System*, R-2904-ICJ, 1982.

Lipson, A. J., *California Enacts Prejudgment Interest: A Case Study of Legislative Action*, N-2096-ICJ, 1984.

Shubert, G. H., *Some Observations on the Need for Tort Reform*, P-7189-ICJ, 1986. (Testimony before the National Conference of State Legislatures, January 1986.)

_____ , *Changes in the Tort System: Helping Inform the Policy Debate*, P-7241-ICJ, 1986.

Jury Verdicts

Carroll, S. J., *Jury Awards and Prejudgment Interest in Tort Cases*, N-1994-ICJ, 1983.

Chin, A., and M. A. Peterson, *Deep Pockets, Empty Pockets: Who Wins in Cook County Jury Trials*, R-3249-ICJ, 1985.

Dertouzos, J. N., E. Holland, and P. A. Ebener, *The Legal and Economic Consequences of Wrongful Termination*, R-3602-ICJ, 1988.

Hensler, D. R., *Summary of Research Results on the Tort Liability System*, P-7210-ICJ, 1986. (Testimony before the Committee on Commerce, Science, and Transportation, United States Senate, February 1986.)

MacCoun, R. J., *Getting Inside the Black Box: Toward a Better Understanding of Civil Jury Behavior*, N-2671-ICJ, 1987.

_____ , *Experimental Research on Jury Decisionmaking*, R-3832-ICJ, 1989. (Reprinted from *Science*, Vol. 244, June 1989.)

_____ , *Inside the Black Box: What Empirical Research Tells Us About Decisionmaking by Civil Juries*, RP-238, 1993. (Reprinted from Robert E. Litan, ed., *Verdict: Assessing the Civil Jury System*, The Brookings Institution, 1993.)

_____ , *Is There a "Deep-Pocket" Bias in the Tort System?* IP-130, October 1993.

_____ , *Blaming Others to a Fault?* RP-286. (Reprinted from *Chance*, Vol. 6, No. 4, Fall 1993.)

Peterson, M. A., *Compensation of Injuries: Civil Jury Verdicts in Cook County*, R-3011-ICJ, 1984.

_____ , *Punitive Damages: Preliminary Empirical Findings*, N-2342-ICJ, 1985.

_____ , *Summary of Research Results: Trends and Patterns in Civil Jury Verdicts*, P-7222-ICJ, 1986. (Testimony before the Subcommittee on Oversight, Committee on Ways and Means, United States House of Representatives, March 1986.)

_____ , *Civil Juries in the 1980s: Trends in Jury Trials and Verdicts in California and Cook County, Illinois*, R-3466-ICJ, 1987.

Peterson, M. A., and G. L. Priest, *The Civil Jury: Trends in Trials and Verdicts, Cook County, Illinois, 1960–1979*, R-2881-ICJ, 1982.

Peterson, M. A., S. Sarma, and M. G. Shanley, *Punitive Damages: Empirical Findings*, R-3311-ICJ, 1987.

Selvin, M., and L. Picus, *The Debate over Jury Performance: Observations from a Recent Asbestos Case*, R-3479-ICJ, 1987.

Shanley, M. G., and M. A. Peterson, *Comparative Justice: Civil Jury Verdicts in San Francisco and Cook Counties, 1959–1980*, R-3006-ICJ, 1983.

_____ , *Posttrial Adjustments to Jury Awards*, R-3511-ICJ, 1987.

Costs of Dispute Resolution

Hensler, D. R., *Does ADR Really Save Money? The Jury's Still Out*, RP-327, 1994. (Reprinted from *The National Law Journal*, April 11, 1994.)

Hensler, D. R., M. E. Vaiana, J. S. Kakalik, and M. A. Peterson, *Trends in Tort Litigation: The Story Behind the Statistics*, R-3583-ICJ, 1987.

Kakalik, J. S., and A. E. Robyn, *Costs of the Civil Justice System: Court Expenditures for Processing Tort Cases*, R-2888-ICJ, 1982.

Kakalik, J. S., and R. L. Ross, *Costs of the Civil Justice System: Court Expenditures for Various Types of Civil Cases*, R-2985-ICJ, 1983.

Kakalik, J. S., P. A. Ebener, W. L. F. Felstiner, and M. G. Shanley, *Costs of Asbestos Litigation*, R-3042-ICJ, 1983.

Kakalik, J. S., P. A. Ebener, W. L. F. Felstiner, G. W. Haggstrom, and M. G. Shanley, *Variation in Asbestos Litigation Compensation and Expenses*, R-3132-ICJ, 1984.

Kakalik, J. S., and N. M. Pace, *Costs and Compensation Paid in Tort Litigation*, R-3391-ICJ, 1986.

_____ , *Costs and Compensation Paid in Tort Litigation*, P-7243-ICJ, 1986. (Testimony before the Subcommittee on Trade, Productivity, and Economic Growth, Joint Economic Committee of the Congress, July 1986.)

Kakalik, J. S., E. M. King, M. Traynor, P. A. Ebener, and L. Picus, *Costs and Compensation Paid in Aviation Accident Litigation*, R-3421-ICJ, 1988.

Kakalik, J. S., M. Selvin, and N. M. Pace, *Averting Gridlock: Strategies for Reducing Civil Delay in the Los Angeles Superior Court*, R-3762-ICJ, 1990.

Lind, E. A., *Arbitrating High-Stakes Cases: An Evaluation of Court-Annexed Arbitration in a United States District Court*, R-3809-ICJ, 1990.

MacCoun, R. J., E. A. Lind, D. R. Hensler, D. L. Bryant, and P. A. Ebener, *Alternative Adjudication: An Evaluation of the New Jersey Automobile Arbitration Program*, R-3676-ICJ, 1988.

Peterson, M. A., *New Tools for Reducing Civil Litigation Expenses*, R-3013-ICJ, 1983.

Priest, G. L., *Regulating the Content and Volume of Litigation: An Economic Analysis*, R-3084-ICJ, 1983.

DISPUTE RESOLUTION

Court Delay

Adler, J. W., W. L. F. Felstiner, D. R. Hensler, and M. A. Peterson, *The Pace of Litigation: Conference Proceedings*, R-2922-ICJ, 1982.

Dungworth, T., and N. M. Pace, *Statistical Overview of Civil Litigation in the Federal Courts*, R-3885-ICJ, 1990.

Ebener, P. A., *Court Efforts to Reduce Pretrial Delay: A National Inventory*, R-2732-ICJ, 1981.

Kakalik, J. S., M. Selvin, and N. M. Pace, *Averting Gridlock: Strategies for Reducing Civil Delay in the Los Angeles Superior Court*, R-3762-ICJ, 1990.

_____ , *Strategies for Reducing Civil Delay in the Los Angeles Superior Court: Technical Appendixes*, N-2988-ICJ, 1990.

Lind, E. A., *Arbitrating High-Stakes Cases: An Evaluation of Court-Annexed Arbitration in a United States District Court*, R-3809-ICJ, 1990.

MacCoun, R. J., E. A. Lind, D. R. Hensler, D. L. Bryant, and P. A. Ebener, *Alternative Adjudication: An Evaluation of the New Jersey Automobile Arbitration Program*, R-3676-ICJ, 1988.

Resnik, J., *Managerial Judges*, R-3002-ICJ, 1982. (Reprinted from the *Harvard Law Review*, Vol. 96:374, December 1982.)

Selvin, M., and P. A. Ebener, *Managing the Unmanageable: A History of Civil Delay in the Los Angeles Superior Court*, R-3165-ICJ, 1984.

Alternative Dispute Resolution

Adler, J. W., D. R. Hensler, and C. E. Nelson, with the assistance of G. J. Rest, *Simple Justice: How Litigants Fare in the Pittsburgh Court Arbitration Program*, R-3071-ICJ, 1983.

Bryant, D. L., *Judicial Arbitration in California: An Update*, N-2909-ICJ, 1989.

Ebener, P. A., and D. R. Betancourt, *Court-Annexed Arbitration: The National Picture*, N-2257-ICJ, 1985.

Hensler, D. R., *Court-Annexed Arbitration in the State Trial Court System*, P-6963-ICJ, 1984. (Testimony before the Judiciary Committee Subcommittee on Courts, United States Senate, February 1984.)

_____ , *Reforming the Civil Litigation Process: How Court Arbitration Can Help*, P-7027-ICJ, 1984. (Reprinted from the *New Jersey Bell Journal*, August 1984.)

_____ , *What We Know and Don't Know About Court-Administered Arbitration*, N-2444-ICJ, 1986.

_____ , *Court-Ordered Arbitration: An Alternative View*, RP-103, 1992. (Reprinted from *The University of Chicago Legal Forum*, Vol. 1990.)

_____ , *Science in the Court: Is There a Role for Alternative Dispute Resolution?* RP-109, 1992. (Reprinted from *Law and Contemporary Problems*, Vol. 54, No. 3, Summer 1991.)

_____ , *Does ADR Really Save Money? The Jury's Still Out*, RP-327, 1994. (Reprinted from *The National Law Journal*, April 11, 1994.)

Hensler, D. R., A. J. Lipson, and E. S. Rolph, *Judicial Arbitration in California: The First Year*, R-2733-ICJ, 1981.

_____ , *Judicial Arbitration in California: The First Year: Executive Summary*, R-2733/1-ICJ, 1981.

Hensler, D. R., and J. W. Adler, with the assistance of G. J. Rest, *Court-Administered Arbitration: An Alternative for Consumer Dispute Resolution*, N-1965-ICJ, 1983.

Lind, E. A., *Arbitrating High-Stakes Cases: An Evaluation of Court-Annexed Arbitration in a United States District Court*, R-3809-ICJ, 1990.

Lind, E. A., R. J. MacCoun, P. A. Ebener, W. L. F. Felstiner, D. R. Hensler, J. Resnik, and T. R. Tyler, *The Perception of Justice: Tort Litigants' Views of Trial, Court-Annexed Arbitration, and Judicial Settlement Conferences*, R-3708-ICJ, 1989.

MacCoun, R. J., *Unintended Consequences of Court Arbitration: A Cautionary Tale from New Jersey*, RP-134, 1992. (Reprinted from *The Justice System Journal*, Vol. 14, No. 2, 1991.)

MacCoun, R. J., E. A. Lind, D. R. Hensler, D. L. Bryant, and P. A. Ebener, *Alternative Adjudication: An Evaluation of the New Jersey Automobile Arbitration Program*, R-3676-ICJ, 1988.

MacCoun, R. J., E. A. Lind, and T. R. Tyler, *Alternative Dispute Resolution in Trial and Appellate Courts*, RP-117, 1992. (Reprinted from *Handbook of Psychology and Law*, 1992.)

Moller, E., E. Rolph, P. Ebener, *Private Dispute Resolution in the Banking Industry*, MR-259-ICJ, 1993.

Rolph, E. S., *Introducing Court-Annexed Arbitration: A Policymaker's Guide*, R-3167-ICJ, 1984.

Rolph, E. S., and D. R. Hensler, *Court-Ordered Arbitration: The California Experience*, N-2186-ICJ, 1984.

Rolph, E. S., E. Moller, and L. Petersen, *Escaping the Courthouse: Private Alternative Dispute Resolution in Los Angeles*, MR-472-JRHD/ICJ, 1994.

Special Issues

Kritzer, H. M., W. L. F. Felstiner, A. Sarat, and D. M. Trubek, *The Impact of Fee Arrangement on Lawyer Effort*, P-7180-ICJ, 1986.

Priest, G. L., *Regulating the Content and Volume of Litigation: An Economic Analysis*, R-3084-ICJ, 1983.

Priest, G. L., and B. Klein, *The Selection of Disputes for Litigation*, R-3032-ICJ, 1984.

Resnik, J., *Managerial Judges*, R-3002-ICJ, 1982. (Reprinted from the *Harvard Law Review*, Vol. 96:374, December 1982.)

_____ , *Failing Faith: Adjudicatory Procedure in Decline*, P-7272-ICJ, 1987. (Reprinted from the *University of Chicago Law Review*, Vol. 53, No. 2, 1986.)

_____ , *Due Process: A Public Dimension*, P-7418-ICJ, 1988. (Reprinted from the *University of Florida Law Review*, Vol. 39, No. 2, 1987.)

_____ , *Judging Consent*, P-7419-ICJ, 1988. (Reprinted from the *University of Chicago Legal Forum*, Vol. 1987.)

_____ , *From "Cases" to "Litigation,"* RP-110, 1992. (Reprinted from *Law and Contemporary Problems*, Vol. 54, No. 3, Summer 1991.)

AREAS OF LIABILITY

Auto-Accident Litigation

Carroll, S. J., J. S. Kakalik, *No-Fault Approaches to Compensating Auto Accident Victims*, RP-229, 1993. (Reprinted from *The Journal of Risk and Insurance*, Vol. 60, No. 2, 1993.)

Carroll, S. J., J. S. Kakalik, N. M. Pace, and J. L. Adams, *No-Fault Approaches to Compensating People Injured in Automobile Accidents*, R-4019-ICJ, 1991.

Carroll, S. J., J. S. Kakalik, with D. Adamson, *No-Fault Automobile Insurance: A Policy Perspective*, R-4019/1-ICJ, 1991.

Hammitt, J. K., *Automobile Accident Compensation, Volume II, Payments by Auto Insurers*, R-3051-ICJ, 1985.

Hammitt, J. K., and J. E. Rolph, *Limiting Liability for Automobile Accidents: Are No-Fault Tort Thresholds Effective?* N-2418-ICJ, 1985.

Hammitt, J. K., R. L. Houchens, S. S. Polin, and J. E. Rolph, *Automobile Accident Compensation: Volume IV, State Rules*, R-3053-ICJ, 1985.

Houchens, R. L., *Automobile Accident Compensation: Volume III, Payments from All Sources*, R-3052-ICJ, 1985.

MacCoun, R. J., E. A. Lind, D. R. Hensler, D. L. Bryant, and P. A. Ebener, *Alternative Adjudication: An Evaluation of the New Jersey Automobile Arbitration Program*, R-3676-ICJ, 1988.

O'Connell, J., S. J. Carroll, M. Horowitz, and A. Abrahamse, *Consumer Choice in the Auto Insurance Market*, RP-254, 1994. (Reprinted from the *Maryland Law Review*, Vol. 52, 1993.)

Rolph, J. E., with J. K. Hammitt, R. L. Houchens, and S. S. Polin, *Automobile Accident Compensation: Volume I, Who Pays How Much How Soon?* R-3050-ICJ, 1985.

Asbestos

Hensler, D. R., *Resolving Mass Toxic Torts: Myths and Realities*, P-7631-ICJ, 1990. (Reprinted from the *University of Illinois Law Review*, Vol. 1989, No. 1.)

_____, *Assessing Claims Resolution Facilities: What We Need to Know*, RP-107, 1992. (Reprinted from *Law and Contemporary Problems*, Vol. 53, No. 4, Autumn 1990.)

_____, *Fashioning a National Resolution of Asbestos Personal Injury Litigation: A Reply to Professor Brickman*, RP-114, 1992. (Reprinted from *Cardozo Law Review*, Vol. 13, No. 6, April 1992.)

Hensler, D. R., W. L. F. Felstiner, M. Selvin, and P. A. Ebener, *Asbestos in the Courts: The Challenge of Mass Toxic Torts*, R-3324-ICJ, 1985.

Kakalik, J. S., P. A. Ebener, W. L. F. Felstiner, and M. G. Shanley, *Costs of Asbestos Litigation*, R-3042-ICJ, 1983.

Kakalik, J. S., P. A. Ebener, W. L. F. Felstiner, G. W. Haggstrom, and M. G. Shanley, *Variation in Asbestos Litigation Compensation and Expenses*, R-3132-ICJ, 1984.

Peterson, M. A., *Giving Away Money: Comparative Comments on Claims Resolution Facilities*, RP-108, 1992. (Reprinted from *Law and Contemporary Problems*, Vol. 53, No. 4, Autumn 1990.)

Peterson, M. A., and M. Selvin, *Resolution of Mass Torts: Toward a Framework for Evaluation of Aggregative Procedures*, N-2805-ICJ, 1988.

_____, *Mass Justice: The Limited and Unlimited Power of Courts*, RP-116, 1992. (Reprinted from *Law and Contemporary Problems*, No. 3, Summer 1991.)

Selvin, M., and L. Picus, *The Debate over Jury Performance: Observations from a Recent Asbestos Case*, R-3479-ICJ, 1987.

Aviation Accidents

Kakalik, J. S., E. M. King, M. Traynor, P. A. Ebener, and L. Picus, *Costs and Compensation Paid in Aviation Accident Litigation*, R-3421-ICJ, 1988.

_____ , *Aviation Accident Litigation Survey: Data Collection Forms*, N-2773-ICJ, 1988.

King, E. M., and J. P. Smith, *Computing Economic Loss in Cases of Wrongful Death*, R-3549-ICJ, 1988.

_____ , *Economic Loss and Compensation in Aviation Accidents*, R-3551-ICJ, 1988.

_____ , *Dispute Resolution Following Airplane Crashes*, R-3585-ICJ, 1988.

Executive Summaries of the Aviation Accident Study, R-3684, 1988.

Employment

Dertouzos, J. N., E. Holland, and P. A. Ebener, *The Legal and Economic Consequences of Wrongful Termination*, R-3602-ICJ, 1988.

Dertouzos, J. N., and L. A. Karoly, *Labor-Market Responses to Employer Liability*, R-3989-ICJ, 1992.

Environmental Litigation: Superfund

Acton, J. P., *Understanding Superfund: A Progress Report*, R-3838-ICJ, 1989.

Acton, J. P., and L. Dixon with D. Drezner, L. Hill, and S. McKenney, *Superfund and Transaction Costs: The Experiences of Insurers and Very Large Industrial Firms*, R-4132-ICJ, 1992.

Dixon, L., *RAND Research on Superfund Transaction Costs: A Summary of Findings to Date*, CT-111, November 1993.

Dixon, L. S., *Fixing Superfund: The Effect of the Proposed Superfund Reform Act of 1994 on Transaction Costs*, MR-455-ICJ, 1994.

Dixon, L. S., D. S. Drezner, and J. K. Hammitt, *Private-Sector Cleanup Expenditures and Transaction Costs at 18 Superfund Sites*, MR-204-EPA/RC, 1993.

Medical Malpractice

Danzon, P. M., *The Frequency and Severity of Medical Malpractice Claims*, R-2870-ICJ/HCFA, 1982.

_____ , *New Evidence on the Frequency and Severity of Medical Malpractice Claims*, R-3410-ICJ, 1986.

_____ , *The Effects of Tort Reform on the Frequency and Severity of Medical Malpractice Claims: A Summary of Research Results*, P-7211, 1986. (Testimony before the Committee on the Judiciary, United States Senate, March 1986.)

Danzon, P. M., and L. A. Lillard, *The Resolution of Medical Malpractice Claims: Modeling the Bargaining Process*, R-2792-ICJ, 1982.

_____ , *The Resolution of Medical Malpractice Claims: Research Results and Policy Implications*, R-2793-ICJ, 1982.

Rolph, E., *Health Care Delivery and Tort: Systems on a Collision Course?* Conference Proceedings, Dallas, June 1991, N-3524-ICJ, 1992.

Product Liability

Dungworth, T., *Product Liability and the Business Sector: Litigation Trends in Federal Courts*, R-3668-ICJ, 1988.

Eads, G., and P. Reuter, *Designing Safer Products: Corporate Responses to Product Liability Law and Regulation*, R-3022-ICJ, 1983.

_____ , *Designing Safer Products: Corporate Responses to Product Liability Law and Regulation*, P-7089-ICJ, 1985. (Reprinted from the *Journal of Product Liability*, Vol. 7, 1985.)

Garber, S., *Product Liability and the Economics of Pharmaceuticals and Medical Devices*, R-4285-ICJ, 1993.

Hensler, D. R., *Summary of Research Results on Product Liability*, P-7271-ICJ, 1986. (Statement submitted to the Committee on the Judiciary, United States Senate, October 1986.)

_____, *What We Know and Don't Know About Product Liability*, P-7775-ICJ, 1993.   (Statement submitted to the Commerce Committee, United States Senate, September 1991.)

Peterson, M. A., *Civil Juries in the 1980s: Trends in Jury Trials and Verdicts in California and Cook County, Illinois*, R-3466-ICJ, 1987.

Reuter, P., *The Economic Consequences of Expanded Corporate Liability: An Exploratory Study*, N-2807-ICJ, 1988.

Workers' Compensation

Darling-Hammond, L., and T. J. Kniesner, *The Law and Economics of Workers' Compensation*, R-2716-ICJ, 1980.

Victor, R. B., *Workers' Compensation and Workplace Safety: The Nature of Employer Financial Incentives*, R-2979-ICJ, 1982.

Victor, R. B., L. R. Cohen, and C. E. Phelps, *Workers' Compensation and Workplace Safety: Some Lessons from Economic Theory*, R-2918-ICJ, 1982.

Trends in the Tort Litigation System

Galanter, M., B. Garth, D. Hensler, and F. K. Zemans, *How to Improve Civil Justice Policy*, RP-282. (Reprinted from *Judicature*, Vol. 77, No. 4, January/February 1994.

Hensler, D. R., *Trends in California Tort Liability Litigation*, P-7287-ICJ, 1987. (Testimony before the Select Committee on Insurance, California State Assembly, October 1987.)

_____, *Reading the Tort Litigation Tea Leaves: What's Going on in the Civil Liability System?* RP-226. (Reprinted from *The Justice System Journal*, Vol. 16, No. 2, 1993.)

Hensler, D. R., M. E. Vaiana, J. S. Kakalik, and M. A. Peterson, *Trends in Tort Litigation:. The Story Behind the Statistics*, R-3583-ICJ, 1987.

MASS TORTS AND ENVIRONMENTAL LIABILITY

Mass Torts

Hensler, D. R., *Resolving Mass Toxic Torts: Myths and Realities*, P-7631-ICJ, 1990. (Reprinted from the *University of Illinois Law Review*, Vol. 1989, No. 1.)

_____ , *Asbestos Litigation in the United States: A Brief Overview*, P-7776-ICJ, 1992. (Testimony before the Courts and Judicial Administration Subcommittee, United States House Judiciary Committee, October 1991.)

_____ , *Assessing Claims Resolution Facilities: What We Need to Know*, RP-107, 1992. (Reprinted from *Law and Contemporary Problems*, Vol. 53, No. 4, Autumn 1990.)

_____ , *Fashioning a National Resolution of Asbestos Personal Injury Litigation: A Reply to Professor Brickman*, RP-114, 1992. (Reprinted from *Cardozo Law Review*, Vol. 13, No. 6, April 1992.)

Hensler, D. R., W. L. F. Felstiner, M. Selvin, and P. A. Ebener, *Asbestos in the Courts: The Challenge of Mass Toxic Torts*, R-3324-ICJ, 1985.

Hensler, D. R., M. A. Peterson, *Understanding Mass Personal Injury Litigation: A Socio-Legal Analysis*, RP-311, 1994. (Reprinted from *Brooklyn Law Review*, Vol. 59, No. 3, Fall 1993.)

Kakalik, J. S., P. A. Ebener, W. L. F. Felstiner, G. W. Haggstrom, and M. G. Shanley, *Variation in Asbestos Litigation Compensation and Expenses*, R-3132-ICJ, 1984.

Kakalik, J. S., P. A. Ebener, W. L. F. Felstiner, and M. G. Shanley, *Costs of Asbestos Litigation*, R-3042-ICJ, 1983.

Peterson, M. A., *Giving Away Money: Comparative Comments on Claims Resolution Facilities*, RP-108, 1992. (Reprinted from *Law and Contemporary Problems*, Vol. 53, No. 4, Autumn 1990.)

Peterson, M. A., and M. Selvin, *Resolution of Mass Torts: Toward a Framework for Evaluation of Aggregative Procedures*, N-2805-ICJ, 1988.

_____ , *Mass Justice: The Limited and Unlimited Power of Courts*, RP-116, 1992. (Reprinted from *Law and Contemporary Problems*, Vol. 54, No. 3, Summer 1991.)

Selvin, M., and L. Picus, *The Debate over Jury Performance: Observations from a Recent Asbestos Case*, R-3479-ICJ, 1987.

Environmental Liability: Superfund

Acton, J. P., *Understanding Superfund: A Progress Report*, R-3838-ICJ, 1989.

Acton, J. P., and L. Dixon with D. Drezner, L. Hill, and S. McKenney, *Superfund and Transaction Costs: The Experiences of Insurers and Very Large Industrial Firms*, R-4132-ICJ, 1992.

Dixon, L. *RAND Research on Superfund Transaction Costs: A Summary of Findings to Date*, CT-111, November 1993.

Dixon, L. S., *Fixing Superfund: The Effect of the Proposed Superfund Reform Act of 1994 on Transaction Costs*, MR-455-ICJ, 1994.

Dixon, L. S., D. S. Drezner, J. K. Hammitt, *Private-Sector Cleanup Expenditures and Transaction Costs at 18 Superfund Sites*, MR-204-EPA/RC, 1993.

Reuter, P., *The Economic Consequences of Expanded Corporate Liability: An Exploratory Study*, N-2807-ICJ, 1988.

ECONOMIC EFFECTS OF THE LIABILITY SYSTEM

General

Johnson, L. L., *Cost-Benefit Analysis and Voluntary Safety Standards for Consumer Products*, R-2882-ICJ, 1982.

Reuter, P., *The Economic Consequences of Expanded Corporate Liability: An Exploratory Study*, N-2807-ICJ, 1988.

Product Liability

Dungworth, T., *Product Liability and the Business Sector: Litigation Trends in Federal Courts*, R-3668-ICJ, 1988.

Eads, G., and P. Reuter, *Designing Safer Products: Corporate Responses to Product Liability Law and Regulation*, R-3022-ICJ, 1983.

_____ , *Designing Safer Products: Corporate Responses to Product Liability Law and Regulation*, P-7089-ICJ, 1985. (Reprinted from the *Journal of Product Liability*, Vol. 7, 1985.)

Garber, S., *Product Liability and the Economics of Pharmaceuticals and Medical Devices*, R-4285-ICJ, 1993.

Hensler, D. R., *Summary of Research Results on Product Liability*, P-7271-ICJ, 1986. (Statement submitted to the Committee on the Judiciary, United States Senate, October 1986.)

_____ , *What We Know and Don't Know About Product Liability*, P-7775-ICJ, 1993. (Statement submitted to the Commerce Committee, United States Senate, September 1991.)

Peterson, M. A., *Civil Juries in the 1980s: Trends in Jury Trials and Verdicts in California and Cook County, Illinois*, R-3466-ICJ, 1987.

Wrongful Termination

Dertouzos, J. N., E. Holland, and P. A. Ebener, *The Legal and Economic Consequences of Wrongful Termination*, R-3602-ICJ, 1988.

Dertouzos, J. N., and L. A. Karoly, *Labor-Market Responses to Employer Liability*, R-3989-ICJ, 1992.

COMPENSATION SYSTEMS

System Design

Darling-Hammond, L., and T. J. Kniesner, *The Law and Economics of Workers' Compensation*, R-2716-ICJ, 1980.

Hammitt, J. K., R. L. Houchens, S. S. Polin, and J. E. Rolph, *Automobile Accident Compensation: Volume IV, State Rules*, R-3053-ICJ, 1985.

Hammitt, J. K., and J. E. Rolph, *Limiting Liability for Automobile Accidents: Are No-Fault Tort Thresholds Effective?* N-2418-ICJ, 1985.

Hensler, D. R., *Resolving Mass Toxic Torts: Myths and Realities*, P-7631-ICJ, 1990. (Reprinted from the *University of Illinois Law Review*, Vol. 1989, No. 1.)

_____ , *Assessing Claims Resolution Facilities: What We Need to Know*, RP-107, 1992. (Reprinted from *Law and Contemporary Problems*, Vol. 53, No. 4, Autumn 1990.)

King, E. M., and J. P. Smith, *Computing Economic Loss in Cases of Wrongful Death*, R-3549-ICJ, 1988.

Peterson, M. A., and M. Selvin, *Resolution of Mass Torts: Toward a Framework for Evaluation of Aggregative Procedures*, N-2805-ICJ, 1988.

Rolph, E. S., *Framing the Compensation Inquiry*, RP-115, 1992. (Reprinted from the *Cardozo Law Review*, Vol. 13, No. 6, April 1992.)

Victor, R. B., *Workers' Compensation and Workplace Safety: The Nature of Employer Financial Incentives*, R-2979-ICJ, 1982.

Victor, R. B., L. R. Cohen, and C. E. Phelps, *Workers' Compensation and Workplace Safety: Some Lessons from Economic Theory*, R-2918-ICJ, 1982.

Performance

Carroll, S. J., and J. S. Kakalik, *No-Fault Approaches to Compensating Auto Accident Victims*, RP-229, 1993. (Reprinted from *The Journal of Risk and Insurance*, Vol. 60, No. 2, 1993.)

Carroll, S. J., J. S. Kakalik, N. M. Pace, and J. L. Adams, *No-Fault Approaches to Compensating People Injured in Automobile Accidents*, R-4019-ICJ, 1991.